Praise for *The Law of Agreement*

"Bravo! Once again, Tony Burroughs is way ahead of his time with a unique perspective about one of the most powerful, yet rarely talked about, phenomena of our lives. *The Law of Agreement* gives the reader an enlightened window on something that rules every aspect of life: the 'agreements' we make with ourselves concerning what we believe about life. This is a must read book for anybody seeking clarity and exponential growth on their life journey."
—Richard D. Blackstone, author of *Nuts & Bolts Spirituality* and *Waking up the Sleepwalkers*

"Tony Burroughs brings visionary information to his readers in clear, comprehensible terms. This book will help you understand and apply the new paradigm principles that will usher you into The Intuition Age. These are skills that pertain to working with energy and awareness, and they will make life much easier for you!"
—Penney Peirce, author of *Frequency* and *The Intuitive Way*

"An awesome book! Tony is a shining gift to the world. He directs you to raise your consciousness, sign a new contractual agreement with yourself, stand in your power, and be the best you that you can be. Follow the call for manifestation and freedom. Journey beyond your own magnificence in this fabulous classic. Well done, Tony!"
—Yvonne Oswald, award-winning, bestselling author of *Every Word Has Power*

i

"I love this book. I make margin notes as I read a book, and I count 45 places where I wrote Yes! or Wow! or Right! or Insightful!, etc. Because it goes a long way toward making the world a better place, *The Law of Agreement* may be one of the most important books you will ever read."

—Wilma E. Bennett, PhD, author of *Vibrations: A Visitor's Guide to Planet Earth*

"I love this book! I wish everyone would read it! Out beyond the law of attraction is the Law of Agreement—having our world work for all of us. This beautiful, powerful, and joy-filled book teaches us very simply and clearly how we can make it happen."

—Jo Ann Rotermund, speaker, workshop leader, and author of *The Forgiveness Habit*

"The beauty of *The Law of Agreement* is in the grace of the writer. Tony Burroughs writing style is joyful; you can feel it when you read his words. Indeed, Tony has given us a moment to pause and recognize that we do not have to agree with the status quo when it is not in our best interests. We can withhold our agreements and know that the changes we seek in our lives can truly be realized by making new agreements. In this way, *The Law of Agreement* has become an operational manual for our daily interactions."

—Karen Monteverdi, author of *Living Consciously in an Ego Driven Society*

The
LAW
of
AGREEMENT

Also by Tony Burroughs

Get What You Want: The Art of
Making and Manifesting Your Intentions

High Lights: The Wisdom of The Intenders

The Vision Alignment Project

The Code, Book 1: 10 Intentions for a Better World

The Code, Book 2: The Reunion: A Parable for Peace

The Highest Light Teachings

The Intenders Handbook: A Guide to the Intention
Process and the Conscious Community

The Intenders of the Highest Good: A Novel

The Bridge: A Magic Book

DVDs and CDs:
The Intention Process: A Guide for
Conscious Manifestation and Community Making

On the Road with the Code (2-DVD or 3-CD Set)

Living by Manifesting (3-DVD or 3-CD Set)

All books, CDs, and DVDs are available at
www.intenders.com and *www.highestlighthouse.com.*

The LAW *of* AGREEMENT

Discover *the* True Power *of* Intention

TONY BURROUGHS

WEISERBOOKS
San Francisco, CA / Newburyport, MA

First published in 2012 by Weiser Books,
an imprint of Red Wheel/Weiser, LLC
With offices at:
665 Third Street, Suite 400
San Francisco, CA 94107
www.redwheelweiser.com

All of the information and personal
accounts herein are based on true events.

ISBN: 978-1-57863-518-4

Library of Congress Cataloging-in-Publication Data

Burroughs, Tony.
The law of agreement : discover the true power of intention / Tony Burroughs.
   p. cm.
Includes bibliographical references and index.
ISBN 978-1-57863-518-4 (alk. paper)
1. Conduct of life. 2. Intention. 3. Attitude change. I. Title.
BJ1581.2.B826 2012
170'.44--dc23
                              2011053146

Cover design by Jim Warner
Interior by Jonathan Friedman/Frame25 Productions

Printed in the United States of America
MAL
10 9 8 7 6 5 4 3 2 1
The paper used in this publication meets the minimum
requirements of the American National Standard for Information
Sciences—Permanence of Paper for Printed Library Materials Z39.48-1992
(R1997).

*This book is dedicated to Mother Earth
and all of Her children*

~May You Rise~

.

Contents

Author's Note

I set out to write a book to help the people of the world. It's a crazy notion, I know, and there are more than a few folks out there who would tell me how futile it is. But I don't believe them. I believe, instead, that there is a light at the end of the tunnel—and we're all on the train, heading for it.

I wrote this for another reason, too. Something deep inside of me bids me to do it. That "something" assures me that this is what I came here to do. Of course, from my personal perspective, I don't know this rationally—*but I do feel it.* I can't help but feel that even the smallest things we do to help our fellow travelers make a difference.

This is the end of my book writing for a while. Great Change is upon us, and where we are going, we won't need books anymore. But we will need *conscience,* and because of that, I have created *The Code,* the Intention Process, the Intenders Circle format for community making, and the Highest Light Teachings for seeing ourselves in our Highest Light. Likewise, I have steadily emphasized in all of my writings the importance of lining ourselves up with the Highest Good. These tools are timeless. You will be able to use them both before and after the Great Change. Indeed, they can be used in any world, anywhere.

So as we round the last bend on our wondrous journey together—a journey that is destined for the stars—I invite you to board our train.

Climb on. It's a great ride. The next stop is the next world. One way or another, I'll see you there.

Prologue

With each day that passes, we are seeing unprecedented changes take place all around us. The old ways, as represented by the insanity in government, economics, media, healthcare, education, and more, will continue to be increasingly cumbersome and eventually fade away, making room for a glorious new world.

It's as if we've been aboard a submarine in wartime and have been submerged in the depths for far longer than we expected. The air inside is fetid and foul, food is running short, and the fear is so intense you can almost touch it. The sailors are edgy and fighting with each other at the drop of a hat. The whole environment inside the sub is ugly and getting worse.

And then, as if summoned by Gabriel himself, the claxon sounds, and the nose of the submarine tips upward. The order has come to rise to the surface. Can you imagine what this is like for the sailors who have been cooped up for so long? What a relief! What a feeling of expansion, as they step on deck and gaze out across the distant horizon! A whole new world, with all its possibilities and wonders, opens up before them!

This is what it's going to be like for us—just as soon as we let go of our old ways. Like the sailors on the sub, that's when we'll begin to rise upward into the light of a new day.

Introduction

A lot of people nowadays are talking about the Law of Attraction and the Law of Allowing. But there is another Law which also begins with the letter A that is just as important—and yet, we in The Intenders are among the very few who are even talking about it. It's called the Law of Agreement and, simply put, it says, *Agreement reinforces reality.* Said another way, *Your agreement with any belief or idea makes it stronger.*

We can easily see how this works by looking at an example. If, for instance, one person believes it's a good idea for everyone to go jump off a cliff, well, then it's not very likely to happen. However, what if one hundred people *agree* that it's a good idea to jump off a cliff? Then the idea gets a little stronger. Taken a step further, if enough people— say 100,000 people—*agree* that cliff jumping is a great idea, pretty soon we're all standing in line at the edge of a cliff waiting for our turn to jump.

It gets even more interesting when we stop to consider that every belief system we have exists only because we agree on it. Indeed, *our agreements are the building blocks of our realities;* they are the very foundation upon which our beliefs are built. Not one belief, large or small, would exist for long without our agreement to it.

Those who seeded us on this beautiful planet knew this, and when they began their colossal project called humanity they sent us here with a certain set of beliefs that would dictate how we would behave. Since our predecessors wanted to keep a certain measure of control over their project (before they turned us loose on our own), they designed these beliefs to be like puppet strings so that they could manipulate us whenever they liked.

Now, however, something unprecedented is happening. Humanity is maturing and is ready to break free and go it alone—and, at the same time, many of the belief systems and ideas we've held on to for eons are not serving us anymore and are rapidly becoming obsolete. This becomes obvious when we look at the tremendous amount of suffering taking place on this planet. Clearly, our inhumanity and our indifference toward each other must stop. It is time for our suffering to come to an end.

"But how do we do this?" you may ask. And the answer is this: *by withdrawing our agreements, one at a time, from any ideas or belief patterns that aren't working for us anymore.*

You see, we all have the option, at any given moment, to agree with what's going on and thus add to it—or to withhold our agreement, and therefore stop reinforcing a reality or system of beliefs that's run its course.

Put still another way, *your agreement is your point of power,* and you can add to or weaken any idea or commonly held belief simply by making a choice. We have with us, in each moment of our lives, the ability *to discern*—to decide whether something is working for us or not—and to choose to *agree* with it and make it stronger, or to say, "Hey, I don't think it's such a good idea for us to jump off that cliff. In fact, cliff jumping never really got us anywhere in the past, and it doesn't look remotely like it's going to give us the results we're looking for in the future. I think I'll pass!"

In the early days of The Intenders, we had a lot of people coming to our Intenders Circles with their dramas. Some of these stories were bona fide issues, but many seemed to be a recurring kind of drama that didn't feel very good to us. As we began to spot these "hip-pocket dramas" (that's what we called them, because it was like they'd just whipped a story out of their hip pocket), we talked about ways of dealing with them that would truly help everyone involved.

First of all, we noticed that these hip-pocket dramas had certain characteristics. We realized that when someone approached us with a hip-pocket drama, we often felt dumped on or drained—and while they seemed to feel a little better, they would move on to the next person and start in on their same drama with them, too. From our point of view, nothing really changed. We didn't feel like we'd done the person with the hip-pocket drama (or ourselves) any good by continuing to agree with them.

So, after talking about it among ourselves, we decided to take a new tack: we decided to withhold our agreement from these hip-pocket dramas and, in this way, not add to their continuation.

Here's what we did: The next time we were approached by someone with a hip-pocket drama and we were beginning to feel ourselves getting embroiled in it, we caught ourselves before lending our agreement, and we simply said, "Ohhh" or

"Mmmm." We didn't even nod our heads, because that would have signified an agreement which would instantly set off an exchange of energy, and then we would have to deal with the emotional charge we'd just taken on—and the person with the hip-pocket drama would just go on to the next person, and the next, and on and on.

In the long run, we got good at saying, "Ohhh" or "Mmmm," and refraining from nodding our heads, so we weren't lending our agreement to their hip-pocket dramas anymore. After that, we felt a lot better, and the people with the hip-pocket dramas began to take a new look at themselves. Many of them ended up making an intention around their hip-pocket drama and came back to us later, expressing their gratitude because their intentions had manifested and their hip-pocket dramas had gone away!

The Law of Agreement will set you free. Used to its fullest, it has the ability and the power to set us all free. We are living on the cusp of great change and are being called upon, now, to make a difference in our world. We can go along with the mainstream media mindset, or we can begin to apply the Law of Agreement in our daily lives and bring about the change we seek.

This book is intended to help you put the Law of Agreement to its highest and best use. I will do my best to show you how the Law of Agreement is working on all levels of your life—from your personal beliefs around money, relationships, and health issues to our long-standing collective, global belief patterns. I will use examples and stories which will help you see the Law of Agreement and its partner, the Law of Adversity, in action so that the next time you are confronted with an idea or a belief that doesn't feel right to you—one that clearly isn't serving you or your fellow men and women anymore—you can choose to exercise your power by using the Law of Agreement.

I assure you that you won't have to wait long. Just turn on the TV, pick up a newspaper, or listen closer to what many of the people around you are saying. Opportunities abound for you to make a difference and apply the Law of Agreement. It could be that all you'll have to do is say, *Ohhh* or *Mmmm,* and hold your head still.

You always have your agreement with you.

The Law of Agreement

Life is like a canvas:
you can paint anything you like on it.
You do not have to paint what someone tells you to paint,
unless you want to.

Or, life is like a garden:
you can plant anything you like in it.
You do not have to plant what someone tells you to plant,
unless you want to.

Times are not hard because someone says times are hard,
times are hard because you've agreed that times are hard;

You are not ill because someone tells you you are ill,
you are ill because you tell yourself that you are ill;

You are not poor because someone tells you you are poor,
you are poor because you tell yourself that you are poor;

You are not part of a group because someone says so;
you are part of a group because you've agreed to it;

And above all…
You are not free because someone else says you are free;
you are free because you tell yourself that you are free.

CHAPTER 1

Those Same Old Tricks

Before we can have true freedom we have to be able to learn from our experiences. This means that we stop repeating the same behavior that has been causing us discomfort and instead change our attitudes and actions. This is how we achieve a different result, one that works better for us and everyone around us.

As we begin to integrate the Law of Agreement into our lives, we will gradually slide out from under the shadows of others who would continue to control us and we'll step into our own sovereign power, independent and strong in the knowledge that each and every one of us is free to create to our heart's content, that we are helped every step of the way, and that nothing can stop us unless we agree to let it.

We can have it all. But first we must be ready to make some changes in the way we look at things. We have to quit falling for some of those same old tricks.

For the past two years I've taken daily walks around the lake near where I live in Colorado. It's my favorite form of exercise, and the magnificent vistas of the surrounding Rocky Mountains provide me with a perfect environment for opening up to new creative ideas.

As is my custom, I walk steadily, never stopping along the way except to take occasional notes and to pet a friendly reddish-brown dog who guards one of the houses by the lake. I call him Rusty, although I doubt that's what his owners named him. He's a collie/chow mix, and he's chained alone to a small doghouse that sits away from the owner's house in the middle of the yard. Rain, shine, or six feet of snow, day in and day out, one thing never changed on my walks: Rusty was always there.

When I first moved into the neighborhood Rusty was younger, and he would bark and jump and run wildly toward me until the chain jerked him to a sudden halt. That didn't stop him, though. Back then, Rusty was lively and full of Spirit. But over the last couple of years something inside him shifted. Now, he's no longer as lively. It's as if he's been beaten down by the boredom and he's resigned himself to living his days at the end of a chain. His Spirit only comes to life in the evening when, for a brief moment, his owner delivers a bowl of food and a few pats on the head before going back into the house.

Then something interesting happened. Just before sunset on a chilly spring evening, I was walking by in my usual way, admiring the last of the season's snow that whitened the peaks in the distance, when Rusty's owner came out with his nightly bowl of food. Rusty jumped up and ran to the length of the chain, only this time, instead of jerking him back into place, the chain broke.

I watched from a distance as Rusty pranced around like never before, free as a bird! At first he stayed well out of the range of his owner, who called and cajoled him for several minutes, all the while cussing the chilly wind and the situation in general. He just wanted to get the dog fed and go back into his warm, toasty house.

Rusty, on the other hand, frolicked and played like a young pup, enjoying his first feeling of freedom in years. His eyes, usually so sullen and sad, sparkled now with a newfound brightness. His Spirit was returning; he had come back to life, and I whispered a silent prayer that he would run away and take his chances out in the world. You see, I'm always trusting that the Universe takes care of us, as long as we intend it for ourselves. To me, it looked like anything would be better than going back to living at the end of a chain.

It was starting to get dark, and as I rounded the end of the lake and turned back toward home, I watched as Rusty's owner went back into the house and came out a minute later holding a bag of special treats high in the air and shaking them loudly. Within moments, Rusty was back on the chain. He was unable to resist the temptation of the tasty nuggets.

The following day, Rusty was there as usual, but his sparkle was gone as he lay there in the dirt with those sad, expressive eyes. Attached to his collar was a new chain, shorter and stronger than the first. He looked horrible, but at the same time there was something different in him, like he hadn't completely forgotten how good it felt to be free the day before. I went up to give him a rub behind the ears, and I was talking to him like I talk to all the animals ("Hi guy! How's it going?" etc.), only this time my curiosity got the best of me and I asked Rusty why he gave up his freedom to live his life chained in the yard, just for the sake of a few treats.

In an instant, Rusty's Spirit, which had seemed so far away only moments before, lit up, and his answer came telepathically into my mind. He said, "Hey Tony, no one's home yet. How about if you unclip this heavy chain from around my neck and we'll see if I fall for those same old tricks again?"

Well … I'd better not tell you what I did.

Humanity is being duped, big-time. Like Rusty, we keep falling for the same old tricks over and over again. In fact, we are being deceived daily, and it seems there is no end in sight. For example, we are being led to believe that our political leaders have our best interests at heart while all evidence points to the contrary: that they care deeply for our children, while they send them off to fight, suffer, and die for reasons which no one can explain without great contradiction; that they are doing their level best to get us out of war while, if they honestly wanted to bring our troops home, the fighting would stop tomorrow and the troops would be home in a week; that they (our elected officials) are the ones who represent us and make decisions on our behalf, while in truth most of the decisions affecting us are made in lavish boardrooms by the businesspeople and bankers who placed our so-called leaders in office and to whom our leaders must answer lest they lose their jobs, or worse. It's just more of those same old tricks . . .

Likewise, we have been *led to believe* that our votes really count, but we neglect to ask ourselves if we were given much of a choice of whom to vote for. With the present two-party system it's obvious that our votes mean very little. All of the people we vote for are beholden to those who give them the money to run their costly campaigns. And, just like with our wars, where both sides of the conflict are funded by the same banks, both political parties in an election are funded by the same banks and businesspeople who couldn't care less who wins because they have all the candidates in their pockets.

And here's a real doozy—we have been *led to believe* that our beautiful Constitution here in the United States is the backbone of our society and that it ensures our fundamental freedoms so we can have a good life. But, almost overnight, our Constitution has been taken away from us. All of the guarantees and tenets which our beloved forefathers meant for us to enjoy have been undermined, diluted, sabotaged, stolen, and stripped away so all that is left is an empty shell which doesn't protect us in the least.

This is not only happening in our government's hallowed halls, it's happening in our businesses as well. We have been *led to believe* that the big businesses that create our products are benevolent. Certainly their advertising tells us so at every opportunity. But is this really true, or is it just more of the same old tricks? For instance, are all of our household cleansers and detergents really good for us? Is it really to our benefit to wear clothing or sleep on bedding that was laundered with those strong-smelling dryer sheets? Is it good for us to breathe in the fumes given off by these things all day and all night? It's doubtful.

Here's another example. Ask yourself, Is it really good for us to continue dumping toxic waste into our precious oceans and then turn around and eat the fish that swam in those waters? Does it make sense for us to line up for vaccines that are supposedly designed to keep us from getting a disease when the disease itself was clearly created and sold to us by the same profit-oriented people who make the vaccines? By the same token, is it wise for us to keep on building more weapons for killing each other, making more violent movies, obsessing about diseases on TV, falling more deeply into debt, manufacturing poisons, and spoiling our waters, our foods, our medicines, our minds . . . ?

It's obvious to almost everyone nowadays that Rome is burning and that We the People are under attack—not from forces outside our borders, but from those whom we voted for, from those who lend us our money, from those who are sworn to protect and defend us, from those who manufacture and sell us our pharmaceuticals, our foods, our household substances, and many of the products we use daily. But what can we do? Faced by such an onslaught, how can we stop ourselves from falling for those same old tricks time and time again? Well, for openers, we can stop feeding the hand that's biting us.

> *If you want to see how a trick works,*
> *withhold your agreement from it.*

The way to make a positive change in your life and in the lives of everyone in our world is to put the Law of Agreement to work on your behalf. The Law of Agreement ensures that as we lend our agreement to any belief, we reinforce it; we make it stronger. Conversely, when we refrain from lending our agreement to an idea that isn't likely to give us the results we're looking for, we dilute it; we weaken its power over us and its power over everyone else simultaneously.

Using the Law of Agreement can change things in a hurry. Now that we are armed with this new information, every belief or snippet of propaganda that comes our way becomes an opportunity for us to take a stand. We can make a difference in our world every time a new idea is presented to us. Whereas in the past we may have been on autopilot and found ourselves nodding or agreeing with propositions without thinking too much about them, now we can utilize the Law of Agreement several times a day. Indeed, we're being called on to make life-changing choices on such a steady basis now that it is important for us to be more alert than ever to what we agree with (or withhold our agreement from), lest we add to that which no longer serves us, to that which is so blatantly obsolete, to that which brings us harm, or to that which we wouldn't want to manifest in a gazillion years.

That having been said, let's take a closer look now at the Law of Agreement, for this is not a subject to be taken lightly. We certainly don't want to keep falling for those same old tricks anymore, especially now that we're beginning to see how they work.

You need not agree with every idea that comes down the pike.

The Old Sleight of Name Game

Currently, we all have an identity. Most often it's a series of words we call our name, as well as a string of experiences related to the body we inhabit. So when someone asks us who we are, we introduce ourselves—typically using the name our parents thought up—and then we tell our story, based on the things that have happened to us while we've been embodied here on Earth. That's the way it's always been done here. But is this the truth? Is this who we really are, or is it the same old Sleight of Name Game designed to keep us from looking deeper into our true identity?

Fortunately, who we think we are is changing. Our perceptions are expanding as the Great Shift of the Ages approaches. The old constricting Sleight of Name Game is giving way to a memory, faint at first, of who we are beyond this Earthly existence. Up to this point we have identified with our name and our body, but now we are starting to see that we are more than that. We are realizing that we are the Being inside our body who thinks and feels and senses intuitively. We are the invisible Essence encased within our skin who has inhabited countless bodies, traversed countless worlds, and taken on countless identities. We have wandered deserts and dimensions, lost ourselves in forests and faraway places, created situations and scenarios that appeared hopeless beyond all understanding.

And yet, here we are, lost again in time and space, but beginning to find ourselves; asleep again in a violent, uncaring realm, but beginning to awaken to who we truly are: a Spirit aglow with love and light, expanding, becoming more, breaking free from our physical containment and stepping forth, fully conscious, into the midst of an unconscious world. It's all part of an organic process that is unfolding, and with each passing day we are letting go of old, encumbered, enslaved parts of ourselves and remembering who we are in eternity.

You can be anyone you want to be. You can have any name you like, but know this: at your core, *you are* all *names and* all *identities*. In order to break free from the old Sleight of Name Game all you have to do is make an agreement with yourself that you are unlimited, that you are vastly more than you previously thought you were. As you make this agreement, an eternal new you will emerge, reveal itself, and expand. It is this expansiveness that you have long awaited.

My name isn't who I am ~ I am much more.
My body isn't who I am ~ I am much more.
My story isn't who I am ~ I am much more.

I only use these things out in the world.
Inside, I am All That Is.

The Vanishing Money Trick

Right now, most people still rely on money as a measure for their happiness. If there is enough of it in their bank accounts and pocketbooks, then they are generally content—and there's nothing wrong with that. But times are spinning fast now, and those with a little foresight can see that the money is steadily being taken out of the hands of the people. A time may come soon when there isn't as much of it around.

It's not that it has to be that way. It's just part of a plan—a plan we all agreed to take part in for the purpose of making ourselves stronger. You might be wondering how we can possibly become stronger if our money is taken away. How could anything but total panic take hold in times of no money? Undoubtedly, the media will make it sound like the whole world has gone mad as these times come upon us. They will roll out the stock footage of lines at the bank and do their level best to scare the heck out of us—and most people will be terrified.

But what about those who aren't terrified? They are the strong ones. They are the ones who won't freeze in fear. They are the ones who everyone else will look to for leadership because they will have already discovered an alternative to money: *living by manifesting.*

Mark these words: *living by manifesting is our next step in life.* It is the hallmark of the new paradigm. It is the threshold we must cross to reach our true freedom. Anyone who would continue to measure their happiness by worthless pieces of paper cannot really be free. Our security comes from within. Our peace of mind is always within reach, and yet we keep it at a distance by clinging to our precious papers and possessions.

Let's look at it another way. Our happiness and peace of mind can be dependent either on money or on our ability to manifest whatever we need. In the first case, where we are reliant on money, there is a whole slew of middlemen—those who print it, those who distribute it, those who regulate it, those who lend it at interest, etc.—and all of these middlemen are constantly dipping their hands into our pockets. In such an imbalanced system we cannot be free because they won't let us. These middlemen have a big stake in our dependence on them. Said another way, they're subtly robbing us of our energy every chance they get.

The alternative is to *live by manifesting*, and it allows us to break free from the middlemen. Our peace of mind can now pass Go, and keep all $200 along the way. And there's something else. Our dignity and self-worth begin to surface again. For how can we hold on to our self-respect as long as we're dependent on another? We can't. Only through learning to live by consciously creating our environment on a moment-by-moment basis can we be free and authentic. And only in freedom and self-respect do we find our strength, our true power.

One morning, years ago, my friend B.J. and I were sitting in the Hawaiian rainforest, taking a break from pruning some avocado trees that were getting too tall to harvest. We leaned back against the trunks of a couple of trees and swatted mosquitoes and drank the last of our coffee. We were surrounded by chain saws, sickles, machetes, and ropes and were sweating profusely. Suddenly, B.J. looked up at me and asked, "What do you think is the biggest difference between us, Tony?"

I didn't quite know where he was going with this, so I gave him a comic answer, "Well, you're taller than me," I said.

He just stared at me. "That's not what I'm talking about," he replied. Then he didn't say anything.

Finally, my curiosity got the best of me and I asked him, "Okay, what is the big difference between you and me?"

"I'm secure," he said. He didn't say the next three words, which, no doubt, would have been, "and you're not!"

I didn't have a chance to respond before he went on. "Yes, I'm secure," he said again. "Whenever I need something to come to me, I simply manifest it. I don't need to go anywhere or do anything special. I just put the Laws of Manifestation to work on my behalf, and everything comes to me."

He was right. I'd seen it happen so many times over the years that I didn't question it anymore. We lived seventeen miles from the nearest town, way off the main road that encircles the Big Island of Hawaii, and time and time again I'd seen him manifest all sorts of things without seeming to have to go anywhere. Often, I would go to bed at night needing a special tool to fix the truck or some other piece of machinery, and when I'd meet him for breakfast the next morning, he'd have "found" the exact tool I needed. It was uncanny.

"So," he went on, "I measure my definition of security by how good of a manifestor I am, by how good I am at getting the things I need to come to me. While you, on the other hand, define and measure your security by how much money you have in your wallet or in your bank account at the moment—and oh, by the way, if your wallet starts to get thin, or your bank account gets a little low, you start to panic!"

I knew he was right. Like most people nowadays, I'd been brought up to believe that if I had a lot of money, I would be secure. The only problem with this line of thinking was that it was becoming more obvious by the day that the money supply was being tampered with, and that our money is systematically being taken out of the hands of all but the few.

"I'm secure," he said, "and it doesn't matter to me whether I've got money in my pocket or not, because if I need something I'll just manifest it. You might want to think about that. Because the time is coming when there might not be as much money around as you'd like. But one thing is certain—"

"—and what's that?" I asked.

"You'll always have your intentions," he said. "No matter what's going on in the world around you, you'll always have the ability to be a conscious cocreator and manifest anything you like. That's where your true security lies—in your proficiency at manifesting, not in how much money you have."

Your money is being used to enslave you— but it doesn't have to be that way.

The Fantastic Foreclosure Fraud

According to the TV and newspapers, many people nowadays are losing their homes or are being forced to move. Foreclosures are increasing as the clouds on the economic horizon darken. For those who are becoming more proficient at manifesting, these changes will not be as dramatic. But the people who are not learning to manifest and create their surroundings deliberately may have some interesting challenges ahead.

At the same time that the news people are sounding their alarms, empty houses abound. As you drive around your towns and suburbs, especially in off-season tourist areas, everything from modest dwellings to fancy villas sit vacant, awaiting someone to move in and be happy. This could be you.

It's interesting that, as we go through our changes, the mindset of the typical landlord is shifting. They are starting to see that it's wiser for them to have someone neat and responsible living in their house, rather than leave it empty. A good caretaker can tend to the upkeep, water the plants, keep an eye out for things that break, pay their own utilities, make the place look occupied, and take care of emergencies. In short, it helps the landlord to have someone living in their home.

That's where you come in. You can manifest a free place to live. You needn't look far, nor should you be affected by the prevailing media hype that says times are hard. Times may be hard for those who aren't learning to live by manifesting, but it is for you to remain centered and realize that you can retain your ability to manifest your own reality, even in the midst of everyone else proclaiming their limitations. They are wedded to the consensus reality, and you are not. You can create anything you desire for yourself and your family, including a free home.

Said another way, you can be empowered in an unconscious, apathetic world. In fact, the instability in the world and the changes you've found yourself going through can actually be seen as gifts. How else would you begin to explore your true power, if it weren't for tough circumstances and challenges? How else would you enhance your ability to manifest things if you hadn't had to deal with some adversity? Seen from a higher perspective, your adversity can lift you up and out of your routines and cause you to reach deep inside yourself for answers to life's most poignant questions. Questions like: Can you create a supportive environment for you and your family while most everyone else feels helpless? Can you revise your definition of "personal security" to include your expertise at manifesting, instead of limiting it to how much money you have in your pockets?

Indeed, the chaos in the world is pushing you toward your own power, and your own creativity—a creativity which includes not just your ability to paint a picture or write a journal, but a broader creativity that encompasses every aspect of life. You can create free housing, all the food you need, friends to help you, enjoyable work, peace of mind, and a lightness of heart, regardless of what your neighbors or the people on the TV are saying.

How do you manifest a home? Begin by sitting in a circle with your family and friends who have a supportive, positive attitude (it's important to remember that it tends to work against you if any of the people in your circle don't believe in what you're doing). Then casually share your ideas about the ideal place you'd like to be living. Make a list. Is it close to town or out in the country? Is it by a body of water? Does it have all the room you need? What is the surrounding topography and vegetation like, etc?

State clear intentions, mentioning every detail you came up with. For instance, say, "I intend that I am living for free in a beautiful house that I love; it is by a lake stocked with fish, in a moderate climate with mountain views, it's close to my work, there's plenty of room for everybody, and it has a fireplace, gardens, etc." Make your list as long or short as you like. (A word of encouragement here: don't limit yourself. Go for the gusto! If you need someplace larger or with special characteristics, you can have it. In fact, if you can manifest one thing, you can manifest another. Why not a free house with all the trimmings?)

After you've expressed your intentions and said that you're grateful in advance for your fabulous free home, take a few moments of silence while everyone in the circle holds a vision in their mind's eye of your new place. See it as clearly as you can, and also see yourself and your family walking around the yard and the kitchen or the living room. Act as if you already have it and do your best to feel how you'd feel at the moment of its manifestation.

Before you break up your circle, line up your intentions with the Highest Good by saying, *"I make these intentions and declare that, in order for them to manifest, they must serve the Highest and Best Good of the Universe, myself, and everyone involved. So be it and so it is! It is done!"*

Now, all you have to do is be open to receive and alert for the opportunities that come your way.

Oh . . . you might be wondering if I've integrated these principles into my own life and manifested a free place to live for myself. The answer is an unequivocal yes! More times than I can count! In fact, right now I'm living rent free in one of the most amazing gems of a house on the planet—a beautiful rustic knotty pine home, right on the river, tucked in among some of the largest, most majestic red rocks you ever saw!

Everyone's fear about money is coming to the surface now. The answer lies in trust. Do you trust in your financial portfolio, or do you trust in a higher power? A higher power has always been there for you, but you have to trust in it. Indeed, if you look back you will see that everything you have needed has always come to you. While many are still filled with the fear of not having anything to fall back on, gifts are being given to those of us who are letting go and opening up. It is a great truth that as you surrender, everything shows up.

Here is a story that came in to The Intenders from our friend Ginnie Hancock from Austin, Texas. It exemplifies the true spirit of living by manifesting.

I read one of the Intender stories last year about a man who intended a rent-free living space. He was down on his luck. I was not down on my luck, but I was new to Austin and renting a room from someone. I really wanted a place of my own for a year. I decided that if he could do it, I could do the same thing. I wanted to pay for the utilities, but no rent.

Two weeks later, one of my new friends had a neighbor that needed someone to live in their home for a year while they traveled on the intercoastal waterways in their new boat. The deal included a dog that I wanted and a truly peaceful environment. This opportunity ends in December. I am already intending a new space so that I can save some money for this next year to make repairs to my home in Houston. There have been other smaller ongoing manifestations, but this was the nicest. I am searching for an active Intenders group out here in Austin. In the meantime, I just want to thank you, as your messages are always helpful and inspiring for me.

—*Ginnie*

As a note of interest, Ginnie's done it again! When her time ran out on the place in the story above, she manifested a choice between two other places for free rent and nominal utilities in Austin and she's living in one of them now. Thank you, Ginnie. What a true inspiration you are!

The Great Disease Deception

It seems like the talk of diseases is everywhere nowadays. You can hardly turn on the tube or talk to a friend without the subject of some disease or another popping up. And, so often, we put ourselves in harm's way by *agreeing* that a disease is real and we could be attacked by it. That's exactly what those who created the disease would like for us to do. They'd like us to buy into the idea that we could catch a disease they just pulled out of their hat because there is big money in it for them. Unfortunately, however, there is only pain and sorrow in it for us, and it is time we began to see how this same old trick works and stop lending our agreement to it. To do that, we will need to take a look at two of the main tools used by those who create our diseases: *"lumping"* and *"naming."*

Lumping is used to describe what happens when we include ourselves with everybody else who has ever had similar symptoms. We "lump ourselves in" with a collective of people who are all appearing to have the same thing going on in their lives. Lumping causes us to disavow our uniqueness and live a lie. We'll talk more about this later.

Naming is how sicknesses and diseases are created. Those who create and profit by our illness (did you ever wonder who they are?) take a grouping of symptoms and give it a name. They know that once we begin to associate a name with those particular symptoms, given enough public relations hype, we'll begin to create it for ourselves.

In this way, if we *agree* that a particular disease, like "the BV," for instance, is running rampant throughout the population, then we run the risk of getting it. *Our agreement with everyone else who believes in it creates the opening for us to experience it.* On the other hand, if a well-meaning friend warns us that "the BV" is spreading, and we choose to withhold our agreement and our belief in it, then we will not be subjected to it.

It's at the moment that we lend our agreement to a belief that we bring it to life.

Perhaps it would be a good idea at this point for us to take a closer look at these subtle "moments of agreement" where we tend to buy into scenarios and situations that aren't serving us anymore. With regard to our health, Mary-Ann's story is one of the best examples of the Law of Agreement in action. This parable is carved right out of today's headlines and is offered, humbly, in times of great darkness to empower those who are able to integrate the message subtly imparted herein.

MaryAnn is an attractive accountant in her late thirties who rides the commuter train to work every day in the city. She is single, friendly, lives with her mother, and is just the kind of person you'd like to meet.

Our tale begins one day when MaryAnn boards the commuter train, sits down in her usual spot, and, across from her, a young man wearing a green camouflage jacket sits down, and he is carrying a birdcage. The birdcage is empty and he sets it on the floor. Then he smiles cordially at MaryAnn, and she, being the outgoing type, returns his smile and nods. An unspoken communication begins, and they both ride the train for fifteen to twenty minutes and get off at their respective stations.

The following day, the young man in the camouflage jacket gets on the train and sits down in the same place as before— only this time he isn't carrying the birdcage. Again, they smile and nod at each other. On this day, however, MaryAnn takes a longer look at him and notices that he appears to be a little pale. She thinks nothing of this at first. But with each passing day, as he sits down across from her, MaryAnn sees that he is growing more and more pale, and he's clearly losing weight and getting progressively weaker. By the end of the week, he has dark shadows under his eyes and is beginning to cough.

This goes on throughout the week until, one day, he does not get on the train. MaryAnn wonders about this, and finally, after several days of not seeing him, her curiosity gets the best of her, and she asks the conductor if he knows what happened to the young man in the camouflage jacket.

"He died last weekend," the conductor says sadly. "It was the BV—the Bird Virus."

MaryAnn mulls this over as she continues on her way to work. When she walks into the lobby of her office, there is a newspaper on an ornate coffee table, and as she passes by it, she can't help but notice the day's headlines. They are a little bigger, and considerably bolder, than normal, and they say, "BV CLAIMS MANY LIVES!"

Immediately, MaryAnn picks up the paper and begins to read the article, which covers the whole top half of the front *page. It describes, in great detail, the same symptoms that the young man on the train had: paleness, rapid weight loss, progressive weakness, circles under the eyes, cough, quick decline, almost always fatal. And, further down, in the next paragraph, it goes on to say that the BV is very contagious and there are "hot spots" where a person is more apt to catch the BV—places like airports, bus terminals, post offices, commuter train stations . . .*

MaryAnn is shocked, and in order to pull herself together before going on to work, she steps into the ladies' room to splash her face with some cold water. As she dries herself off with a paper towel, MaryAnn looks in the mirror and notices a faint shadow taking form under her eyes! In a state of near panic, she sits at her desk for the next several hours trying to concentrate on her bookkeeping, but with very little success.

At home that evening, while her mother is in the kitchen preparing their evening meal, MaryAnn flips on the six o'clock news and it is ablaze with stories about the BV. The excited anchor-woman is describing all the symptoms in even greater detail while the screen is filled with footage of sick people, noisy, packed hospital emergency rooms, and sorrowful statistics of all sorts.

After dinner, MaryAnn is feeling weak and goes to bed early. The next morning, she feels so bad that she can't even go to work. She remains bedridden for three days, with all of the BV symptoms, one by one, beginning to manifest themselves. On the fourth day, her mother calls a doctor.

The doctor, though compassionate, is obviously distracted and in a hurry and is only too quick to make his diagnosis. "I'm afraid she has the BV," he tells MaryAnn and her mother, and he prescribes some pills that are meant to make MaryAnn's last days more comfortable. After this he says that there's not much more he can do, and he leaves.

Three days later, thinking that her beautiful daughter is going to die at any moment, MaryAnn's mother calls a priest. But the priest her mother calls is not your average priest. He is a new-paradigm priest, and he knows only to see the wellness—never to see the sickness. He knows how to hold the light for others while they are unable to hold it for themselves. And he sees MaryAnn in her Highest Light, completely well, happy, healthy, whole, and full of life. The priest holds this vision in his mind regardless of what anyone else tells him about her. He holds the template of her in her Highest Light—no matter what! Then he shows MaryAnn's mother how to hold that same vision in her imagination, so she sees her daughter perfectly well and happy. He also teaches MaryAnn how to hold that image for herself.

Before the priest leaves, he places his hands on MaryAnn's head for a moment, then on her neck, then on her heart, and finally he massages her shoulders gently. As he does this, he sends the light and love of God through his hands to every cell, every atom, every molecule, every strand of DNA in Mary-Ann's body (you can call it Reiki, Deeksha, Ilahinoor, Divine Light Transmission, Oneness Blessing—they all work). He fills her entire body, from head to toe, with Light!

And then he leaves . . .

Two hours later, MaryAnn is out of bed for the first time in two weeks. The next day, she is puttering casually around the house. Three days after that, she's shopping. And later the following week, she is back at work—happy, healthy, and hummin' with life—all because she ran into a new-paradigm *priest: someone who knew how to hold the light for others, regardless of any and all evidence to the contrary!*

But wait . . . there's an epilogue to our tale. One morning, a week after MaryAnn went back to work, she was sitting on the commuter train when guess who boarded it and sat down right across from her? The young man in the green camouflage jacket! He wasn't dead at all. The conductor was entirely mistaken. The young man was just overworked. He was fine.

So, let's take a closer look at MaryAnn's story with new paradigm eyes. There were several places in it where Mary-Ann bought into the sickness instead of the wellness. Can you name a few?

Here they are, gently encoded for you: *rotcudnoc eht; reppapswen eht; swen vt ylthgin eht; rotcod eht; rorrim eht; .cte.*

As a final note: Isn't it interesting that every time Mary-Ann bought into the sickness and, therefore, created it for herself (our thoughts create our world), she also had the option to remain neutral or to withhold her agreement from it and go, *Ohhh,* or *Mmmm* and therefore not manifest it for herself?

We are amazing cocreators who have literally stepped down from the throne of our own power by "buying into" the ideas and beliefs that were placed here by someone else and which clearly do not serve us anymore. But now, with the help of the Law of Agreement, we can begin to spot more and more instances when these questionable beliefs are being presented to us, and we can exercise our option to withhold our agreement completely—thus, holding them at bay. In doing so, we begin to see through the Great Disease Deception and bring the light of truth into our lives.

So now that we've had a moment to digest MaryAnn's story, let's go back and look at the topics of *lumping* and *naming* in greater detail so we can see how they work in tandem to affect us. It is a fundamental truth, from a higher perspective, that each and every one of us is a unique Being, and whatever physical imbalance we're experiencing at any given time, whether it is a slight pain or a persistent ailment, is unique unto us. Indeed, we have different parents, different schooling, different genetics, different fingerprints, different cereals for breakfast, and entirely different experiences than everyone else. But when we *lump ourselves in* with everyone else who ever had similar symptoms by agreeing with the doctor, the newscaster, or the conductor on the train who says that we have or could catch the BV, we do ourselves a tremendous disservice—and we set the stage for us to have to live out the manifestation of our beliefs.

You see, our mind is much more active and astute than we give it credit for, and it knows the symptoms of every disease in the *Physician's Desk Reference.* Since we were young children, we were taught all about diseases in our schools and from the TV, and most of us never realized that just by hearing the name of a disease, our mind, if allowed to go unchecked, will send messages to the body to begin replicating the symptoms associated with the disease. (That's why we in The Intenders have always refrained from the naming of sicknesses and diseases.)

Said another way, when we believe a doctor or someone else when they tell us we have a particular disease, we *lump ourselves in* with everyone else who has ever had similar symptoms to ours, not realizing that our mind, in its infinite wisdom, will begin to send messages to our body telling it to create the symptoms we are believing in. And, since our thoughts are always creating our experiences, our body will immediately comply with the mind's wishes and begin to manifest the disease we believe we have.

This is how diseases are created. When we *agree* that diseases exist, we make them stronger. Isn't it time for us to consider becoming much more careful about what we *agree* upon, lest we create it?

Many years ago the Rosicrucians set up experiments to show us the power that our thoughts have upon our body. They hypnotized people and then approached them with a normal pencil or pen, telling them it was a burning hot poker, like a branding iron. Then they touched the pen to the person's arm, and guess what? The person immediately cried out in pain and a large reddish blister began to form. Almost instantaneously, the arm took on all the physical characteristics of having really been burned.

Stories like this have been hidden from us, but their message is clear: We human beings tend to be very open to suggestions, and it serves us well to remember that we are each unique. Likewise, it does not serve us to believe everything that people may tell us about ourselves. Not only could their suggestions be entirely wrong, but if we believe them, we run the risk of manifesting all sorts of things we're apt to wish we'd stayed away from.

Remember, it is we who create our reality, not somebody else—unless we give them our agreement.

I have a good friend, Q, who lives in the mountains of Northern California. He's been an Intender for quite some time and has followed my work closely for many years. Q (that's his real nickname) calls me every couple of months to see what I'm up to. I even stayed in his mountain cabin a few summers ago for a short while.

One day, I received a call from him. He wanted to know where I was so we could get together soon. As it happened, another friend of his had given him a camper van similar to mine, and he was readying himself to take up the gypsy life. Since Q was in California and I was in Florida at the time we agreed to meet up in the Midwest in a couple of months.

As it turned out, that wasn't the real reason Q had called me. During the course of our conversation, he mentioned, almost casually, that the doctors had recently told him he had "the big C" and he was intending to find a Native American healer in Sedona. Did I know of one?

I gave him the name of a friend in that area, and we continued chatting lightly for a few more minutes and hung up. It took me less than five minutes to digest what had just happened and I called him right back.

"Q, I just couldn't get what you told me out of my mind. Is it alright with you if we talk about what the doctors said for a few minutes?"

"Of course, Tony."

"Well, from my point of view, Q, you have a choice to make here. Are you going to go along with what the doctors told you and therefore create it for yourself—or do you choose to withhold your agreement with them and create something else for yourself?"

He was silent, thinking, so I went on.

"The way I see it, my friend, is that they are selling you something...but you don't have to buy it if you don't want to." He chuckled a bit. "Tony, you're right about that. They make it all sound so convincing."

"Yes, they do—but there's an inherent lie in what they're trying to sell you. Even though they generally mean well, they're just guessing, and they can be very convincing about it. The truth is that you just have whatever you have, and there's no need whatsoever to give it a name. In fact, there's never any need to give a name to any physical imbalance we're experiencing."

"Hmmm..."

"That's right, my friend. What you may or may not have is unique unto you. It's not exactly like anything anybody else ever had. Just because you may have a few symptoms that are similar to what others may have had doesn't mean that you have what they had. If, however, you buy into what the doctors are selling you, you will have to live it out. If you continue to go along with them and keep telling me and your other friends that you have this 'big-named disease,' then each time you do this, you are reinforcing the disease. You're making it stronger. Understand?"

"Yes, I see that now. Thanks for the reminder." There was a note of pure gratitude in his voice. I was so glad I called him back.

"Right, Q, I know you know this, so it is just a reminder. And, in the meantime, if it's alright with you, I'm going to see you only in your Highest Light. Regardless of what you or anyone else tells me about you, I'm going to see you well and happy and living your life to the fullest. I'll hold the template of perfect health for you; in fact, I am anchoring that template onto this Earth as we speak. And no matter what anyone tells me about their body or their imbalance, I'm only going to see them in their highest state of health. Since our thoughts create our experiences, I'm only holding the thought of optimum wellness for everyone I meet, and that includes you. Is that okay with you?"

"Absolutely!" he said. He was sounding brighter already.

"Great, Q. Because there isn't any sickness on this Earth that hasn't been healed. They've all been healed at one time or another. What you think you have isn't any different. All you have to do is keep your thoughts and words totally focused on your wellness, and that's what you'll create. And if you forget, call me and I'll remind you. Is it a deal?"

"It's a deal!" he said, and I distinctly heard the smile in his words. It was like a great relief had come over him. He obviously felt better, and you know what? When I hung up the phone, I felt a whole lot better too.

This conversation took place several years ago, and Q and I still keep in touch. He's in Vermont now and doing fine.

When you really stop to think about it, one of humanity's strangest predilections is that we look for confirmation for our ailments. We look to see what happened to everybody else who has experienced similar symptoms to ours, and in doing so, we put ourselves in harm's way. What many people don't realize is that just because somebody else developed a chronic condition after showing similar symptoms to ours doesn't mean the same will happen to us.

We are all dealing with toxic thoughts, substances, and experiences in our world that may or may not present us with short-term aches, pains, bumps, zits, and so forth. It's a part of life nowadays. What we oftentimes forget, however, is that a great many of the things we think are "wrong" with us are only temporary. They'll go away by themselves in a short time if we leave them alone. Sure, sometimes we'll need to adjust our diet or our work habits for awhile, and that is natural. But it's unnatural for us to look too deeply for confirmation or validation for the causes of our ailments. In fact, we run certain risks when we delve too deeply, parading every disease imaginable before us in a quest to find out the cause of an ache or pain. We tend to make things chronic that would have only been temporary.

You see people do this all the time. They'll get a new bump somewhere on their body and begin to mull over all the reasons as to how it could possibly have gotten there. They'll check out magazines, talk to friends, surf the Internet, and have doctors run test after test as they search frantically to find out what happened to others who also had similar bumps. In order to validate their own theories (which are growing rapidly now), they'll even resort to going out of their way to find coincidences. For example, while walking through a popular coffee shop, they might notice a magazine sitting on the rack with an article in it that describes what happened to a person who had a similar bump—and lo and behold, they treat this as a confirmation for their own condition, thus making it worse.

Fortunately, there are a couple of good antidotes for the toxicity in our world today. First, we can always remind ourselves that we are creating whatever we put our attention on, and that when we dig too deeply in search of explanations for our aches and pains, we run the risk of bringing other possibilities into the picture that have nothing to do with our original situation. Instead, we can tell ourselves that we are fine by saying, "I am FINE!" We can also see ourselves in our Highest Light and withdraw our agreement from any sickness scenarios. According to the Law, as we envision ourselves being happy, healthy, balanced, and whole, that is what we will create.

Second, we can trust that whatever is bothering us is only temporary and will go away on its own very soon. The shamans and medicine men of old knew that prayer, intention, and fasting healed almost everything in a few days. It could be that instead of spending our precious energy in search of confirmation for what ails us, we could stop eating or begin a Master Cleanse to rebalance the pH of our blood, retire into a quiet place where we can be alone for awhile, and call on the Highest Good to help us.

Please understand that I am not saying that everyone instantly gets well through using these methods—some people need to experience their imbalance to the fullest in order to learn something from it. I am also not saying there is anything wrong with going to a medical practitioner for certain treatments. If you believe that a doctor will help you, then, by all means, that is the route you should follow. If you have a broken bone or need to have a cut stitched up, doctors are the experts and can be of great help. But when it comes to diagnosing sickness, it's a guessing game and we're still in the medical dark ages. It's easy to come out of a hospital or doctor's office nowadays feeling worse than when you went in. On the other hand, if you can bring yourself to believe in the power of prayer, intention, fasting, pH balancing, and seeing yourself in your Highest Light, you have a just as good or better chance of getting rid of your health challenges than if you were to use any of the typical remedies prescribed by the credentialed medical establishment. That's a universal fact.

Here is a comment that my friend, artist, and holistic nutritionist Kass Callaghan sent to me:

Here is a simple little thing that works for me whenever anyone tries to give me bad news. I just reverse what they said to exactly the opposite in my mind. If they say this and that is so bad, I just change the subject in my mind to see the opposite. I can have an entire conversation with someone who thinks they are laying gloom and doom on me when in fact they are not. When my opinion is asked for in the conversation I respond from this more positive perspective. And here is what happens then: the conversation turns to one of a positive nature all on its own.

So, every time you feel that it is time to visit your doctor, try this. If he begins to tell you that you are sicker or whatever, in your mind reverse that and tell yourself he just told you that you were perfectly healthy and getting even more healthy every day. And if he suggests more tests for you, and you feel you must oblige, then just tell yourself these tests are to test their equipment and not you because you are perfectly healthy. Just reverse everything he says in your mind. And when you see him next time just look at him like he is your favorite friend in the whole world and you are happy to see him. You will soon see the conversations with him begin to change to your way of thinking and feeling. He will be picking up on your energy and feelings and that in turn will alter his.

—Kass Callaghan
Sonoma, California

Playing Catch

One of the most pervasive of all the same old tricks being shoved at us is contagion. Also known as *playing catch,* it suggests that we can catch sicknesses from other people. While this is true, it's only under one condition: *we have to believe that we can.*

It's no different than when we were kids and someone said, "Hey, let's play catch!" and they threw the ball at us. In most cases, we couldn't resist reaching out and catching it. In real life, however, it's not wise for us to reach out and catch every ball that comes our way. We serve ourselves and all those around us better if we simply let the ball go by and go on about our day.

Playing catch describes the entire foundation upon which contagiousness, or the *germ theory of disease,* is built. It depends 100 percent on our gullibility, on our openness to reach out and believe in ideas that don't serve us but which engender huge profits for those who have a vested interest in them.

Germ theory is just a theory—it is not a fact at all. It would have us believing that a bunch of little bitty bugs are out to get us. We are shown pictures of these little bugs swimming around in Petri dishes or on microscope slides, and we are told that what we are seeing is very dangerous. To make matters worse, we are also told that if we come into contact with someone else who has a few of these bugs in them, then we could catch whatever sickness they have. This ploy has been used for thousands of years, but its days are numbered as we begin to delve deeper into how it all works.

For germ theory to work, we have to forget that our thoughts, and not a bunch of little bugs, are creating our experiences.

Furthermore, we have to give our power over to those who make these conscience-less suggestions, and in doing so, two things occur: first, we open ourselves to having to deal with all sorts of maladies, and second, we separate ourselves all the more from our fellow men and women—and that is the most harmful thing we could allow to happen, for it leads to a scenario where, if the powers that be have their way, we would all end up wearing face masks, rubber gloves, and all sorts of protective clothing in order to keep ourselves apart from each other. The sad part is that this agenda is being pushed on us at a time when it is clearly to our great advantage to explore ways of coming together in community, instead of allowing ourselves to be divided even further.

Here's the point: We have the choice about what we believe in. *We have the choice about what it is that we create with our everyday thoughts and words.* Just because the media or our coworkers and close friends have bought into the game of playing catch doesn't mean we have to agree with them. Instead, we can withhold our agreement and therefore remove ourselves from harm's way. We can choose to see ourselves healthy, happy, and living our lives to the fullest, and, by the Law, that is what we will create.

This brings up perhaps one of the most important questions we can ask ourselves: What is it that we really want to create? Do we want to believe the stories about the little bitty bugs and continue to create a world of suffering and sickness? Or do we want to stand strong in our integrity in the face of all the ruses and suggestions? We always have the ability to see ourselves in our Highest Light, filled to the brim with light, love, and life, and thus create that for ourselves.

Here's another example of playing catch from a fellow Intender:

I have a friend who went to the doctor's office awhile back and got sicker as a result. What happened was that she was made to stand in line for a long time with a crowd of other sick people, and one of them sneezed in her direction. She left right away and came home that night to tell the whole story about how it felt bad at the doctor's office, and about the peril she didn't realize she had put herself in. I explained to her that she didn't have to believe that way, but she didn't hear me.

Two days later, she went to bed with all sorts of symptoms. Only after she got well was I able to explain to her about how she manifested the whole experience for herself by believing in old-paradigm ideas about catching things from people who are coughing and sneezing. From that perspective, the whole situation, including her time in bed, became a blessing because she's been perfectly well ever since.

—Lindy McCormick
San Diego, California

When people realize that their thoughts and their words are creating their future, then they can begin to create a better future for themselves.

The Age-Old Old-Age Agreement

What about aging? As we shift from the old ways of living to the new ways, we find ourselves learning to stretch our thinking processes beyond their old boundaries. Now that we know our body will physiologically follow the dictates of our mind, we are no longer served by many of our old thinking and speaking habits, especially those surrounding aging and how we talk about it.

Over the course of human history, we have lived long and we have lived short. It wasn't too long ago that the average human lifespan was under fifty years of age; now it's over eighty, and going up. These figures tell us about our collective tendencies, but they don't explain the anomalies or our potentials.

Remember Methuselah, the oldest man mentioned in the Bible, who lived for nearly a thousand years? Or St. Germain, who never seemed to age even after being seen decades later by friends who knew him well? Or how about the Indian saint Mahavatar Babaji, or the Ancient Egyptian god Thoth, both of whom are still supposed to be around? People have seen these men on too many occasions for us to dismiss their stories lightly. What are they doing that we're not?

To begin with, these long-lifers aren't buying into the collective consensus reality by associating certain physical manifestations with their age. For example, it's doubtful that they believe we tend to lose our memory as we get older or that when we reach certain milestones, everything slows down for us. No, they're a lot more careful about how they create their future. They don't give voice to their limitations. You'd never hear them say something like, "I think I'm going to need eyeglasses now that I'm getting older," or "The older I get, the harder it gets." Instead, they are marching to a different drummer, one that stays alert and positive in all situations.

Many masters have taught that once our perceptions are enhanced and we gain access into the invisible worlds that surround us, we get to the stage where we can literally create the form, shape, and age of our bodies that we choose. Such is our birthright as Spiritual Beings occupying a human form. Once we learn to rejuvenate ourselves and create the body of our choosing, the masters tell us we'll look back at these times and wonder how we could have ever participated in any conversations that limited us so drastically. They say that glib catchphrases, especially those which describe us as we get older, won't be a part of our vocabularies like they are now.

The body that you choose can be yours.

The Storm and Sickness Seasons

When you have a lot of people agreeing and envisioning the way things will be, then that's the way things will be. There is tremendous power in a group of people focused on a common objective. It works within a positive environment, such as in an Intenders Circle where everyone is holding a vision of everyone else's intentions being manifested, and it works just as easily within a negative environment, such as when we're creating fearful weather conditions or seasonal sicknesses for ourselves.

You don't have to look very far to see that our weather is being tampered with. Those in power would have us believe that the weather is out of our control, that we are at the mercy of the storms and climatic changes. But this simply isn't so. In fact, it's just the opposite. It is we who create every aspect of our environment, including the weather. We've just forgotten about it.

So, here's a gentle reminder. Night after night, in homes all across the globe, the weathermen and women prance around the TV screen telling us what the weather is going to be like. Much in the same way that drug companies create flus and sicknesses of all sorts by describing them and pulling flimsy "facts" out of thin air, the weatherpeople describe the coming weather changes, and, if we believe them, we add to the creation of the bad weather.

Can you imagine the power in that? Millions of people holding the same thought is an awesome prospect in itself. And now, with all the satellite imagery graphics, the friendly weatherperson can even have us picturing large weather systems impacting whole parts of the planet. This is the point where we give up our power and hand it over to someone else. People everywhere either forget or simply don't realize that their thoughts are creating their world. They *agree* with the pictures they see on TV and waste no time telling everyone they run into that a storm is on the way.

That's how storms, flus, or any other mass events are orchestrated. And if that isn't enough, now the weatherpeople have even created storm and sickness "seasons" in order to get us primed and ready to experience bad times. Clearly, the weatherpeople are now doing the bidding of the big pharmaceutical companies by talking about seasonal sicknesses. What can we do?

Two things. First, we can turn their weather reports off and *withhold our agreement* every time someone tells us a storm or sickness season is on the way. Simply refuse to believe it. In that way, we are not reinforcing the event.

Second, we can become proactive by using the weatherperson's satellite images of storms against them. Whenever we see the great masses busily creating a storm, we can become a Storm Steerer. For instance, instead of believing that a hurricane is going to follow the course described by the anxious weatherperson, we can use the wondrous lightworking tool we call our imagination and, in our mind's eye, we can steer the storm out to sea, or see it dissipating into nothing before it has a chance to hit land. Technologies once hidden from us are now revealing that the scalar waves you see on the horizon, like heat coming off the pavement in the distance, are directly affected by human intention. We can literally intend our weather to change, and it will!

So what if enough Storm Steerers pictured the storms going away? They would go away. I've seen huge tropical storms move away from the Big Island after fifty Intenders intended it. Can you imagine what would happen if thousands of people from all over the globe became Storm Steerers? It would change everything—not just with the weather and the sickness seasons, but with the way we create our entire world.

You can create your life to be any way you want it.

The Old Separation Scam

At a time when things in our world are becoming more unstable by the day, and our core values and beliefs are clearly no longer working for us like they used to, we in the Intenders offer an intention—that we let go of our old, unloving ways and find a more equitable way of managing our world than we've had in the past.

At present, the community of mankind is still run by businessmen and self-serving politicians, and it's easy for people to get all riled up about the political scene. However, it's wise to keep politics in perspective. *Politics, by definition, is the art of controlling and manipulating people,* and to the extent that we spend our precious energy talking on and on about who's going to win, or what changes a politician says they're going to make, we are allowing ourselves to be distracted and steered away from how good it would be if we all worked together as One.

Politicians typically make use of what we call the Separation Scam to keep control over us, and it's one of the oldest tricks in the book. The Old Separation Scam, also known as the Us Versus Them Game, the Divide and Conquer Ruse, and the Disappearing Oneness Trick, is so much a part of our lives that we almost take it for granted. And yet, at the same time, it is becoming more obsolete by the day as people everywhere begin to see how it works.

The Old Separation Scam began for each of us when we were very young and trusted those who were older and bigger than us to steer us in the right direction. Little did we know that many of our elders had agendas of their own, and the best way they could find to get us to do their bidding was to pit us against each other. In other words, without conscience, many of our parents, teachers, and media people indoctrinated us as small children—when we didn't know any better—and they taught us to separate ourselves into camps based on where we lived, what we looked like, how much money we had, what we believed in, and so on. We were told to identify with our nation (I am an American, Lithuanian, South African, etc.), our race (I am white, black, red, yellow, and all mixes in between), our class (I am rich, middle-class, Brahmin, priestly, serf, slave, etc.), our religion (I am a Christian, a Jew, a Hindu, a Moslem, a Buddhist, etc.), and so on. The list of camps is seemingly endless.

The Separation Scam requires constant maintenance because it relies on us being distracted every step of the way from our true nature, which is Oneness with everyone and everything. We must never be allowed to experience our Oneness, because when we do, we'll find out that it feels so good we'll never lend our *agreement* to the Old Separation Scam again.

That's when we'll stop turning the reins of our own empowerment over to someone else and start to control our own lives. In truth, the solutions for today's challenges will never come from the political arena. Today's politicians, without exception, are bought and sold, lock, stock, and barrel. Like puppets, they do the bidding of private masters or else they wouldn't be standing on the podium in front of us. Regardless of who wins an election, nothing of importance will change—and to think otherwise is only to delude ourselves further.

The more you align yourself with the Family of One, instead of a country, race, class, religion, or party, the sooner your fears will subside and the closer you will come to experiencing your greatest happiness.

Programming Our Preschoolers

Did you ever wonder how we got to be the way we are? How did we become so militaristic, so obsessed with our allegiance to a nation to the point where we are willing, even eager, to fight, kill, and die on its behalf? The answer lies in the programming we received when we were in preschool, and even before. We were conditioned and brainwashed from the time we were first beginning to formulate our ideas about the way the world works. The powers that be on this Earth knew that if they began disciplining us at such an early age, it would be very hard for us to change our beliefs and our perspectives later on.

Allegiance is a very powerful form of agreement. Oftentimes, it involves us obligating ourselves to institutions with agendas—agendas that we more often than not had no part in creating. The Toltec teachings are very clear about these kinds of agreements. Their elders knew that it was unwise for their people to hold on to an allegiance or agreement that they didn't personally make of their own free volition. The Toltecs didn't believe they had to honor agreements that were made under duress or when they were so young that they didn't know any better. Therefore, they only honored agreements that they had consciously taken part in making.

Let's take a look at a present-day example of the kind of allegiance the Toltecs would likely rescind. Did you ever wonder why so many of our young people are excited about going off to war? That inclination isn't something we are born with. If you think about it, it runs completely counter to the path of human evolution. In truth, we are set up to experience the fullness of life, to enjoy being a toddler as well as an elder. Our evolution bids us to learn as we grow, and each stage of life furthers the possibility for us to become something greater, something magnificent.

Why would we deliberately want to do anything to cut our lives short? Why are we so ready to take part in the mass hysteria we call war? Obviously, the answer lies in what happened to us when we were very young. From the time we were so small that we didn't know any better, we were conditioned to be soldiers. We were spoon-fed the idea that there are nasty enemies out to get us, and there is some strange kind of glory in fighting and dying for our countries. We were led to think that it was honorable to kill and be killed in the name of patriotism.

It is truly amazing that humanity continues, to this day, to accept these malicious ideas. Can you imagine the tremendous effort it takes to keep people going against the grain of their own natural evolution? It involves a massive, constant bombardment of our minds at every level of life. Rarely do we find ourselves in a place where the reminders of war, enemies, fighting, and patriotism leave us alone. Images of fighting, killing, and dying are ever-present on billboards and television, in movies, newspapers, history books, popular novels, and more. And we, like good soldiers, seldom question it all. It's as if we have been dumbed down and brainwashed—and, in fact, that is exactly what is happening.

Indeed, we must ask ourselves: who gains from all of the killing? Why would anyone want to make fighting and dying sound like a picnic in the park? Why would anyone take the trouble to teach our preschoolers that military disciplines will give them fulfillment in their lives? And why would We the People continue to keep *agreeing* with it all?

It's a horrid, insane cycle, and it must be broken. Not one more child need be wounded or killed in the name of a contrived "enemy." Not one more weapon need be forged, nor bomb dropped, nor home destroyed. Clearly, a sickness runs through the once hallowed halls of power, and anyone who would inflict the pain and death of war on our youth is some strange sort of child abuser. They get their kicks out of all the suffering, or else they would stop doing it immediately.

I understand that these are not popular points of view; but if nothing ever changes, we will continue to disavow our children, dishonor their evolution, and dispatch them, like cattle in slaughterhouse pens, to the fields and deserts of death. Make no mistake, I am not recommending that you oppose our rulers and leaders. Opposition only creates more opposition. The days of our opposing others are fast coming to an end as the Old Separation Scam comes to light. No, I am simply suggesting that you withdraw your allegiance and your agreement from any belief, idea, system, institution, or person who advocates the harming of our precious children.

I am suggesting that you take a stand for peace, once and for all, by rewriting your past. You can rewrite your past by going back in your mind to the time when you were a preschooler and recalling when a bigger person was telling you that you should join in with the rest of your countrymen and women in defending yourself against your "enemies" by preparing yourself to be a soldier.

I am intending, here and now, that we all stand up to those bigger people in our minds, as well as those in our outer world, and tell them to take a hike. Tell them that we don't believe them anymore, and that we're here on Earth to love our fellow men, not bring harm to them. I am intending that we all begin to rescind our national allegiances now that we've seen the utter insanity in continuing to honor them, and to withdraw our agreement and support from anyone who creates enemies, builds bombs, makes war, or turns our innocent youth into killing soldiers. I am intending that we all begin to rewrite our past so we are free to experience peace now. Our children will thank us.

When I was in kindergarten I remember standing up, placing my hand on my heart, facing the flag, and repeating the Pledge of Allegiance with all the other kids. I didn't really understand what was going on, but I was certain that if I didn't go along with the teachers I would be in big trouble (or at least I wouldn't get my chocolate milk and graham cracker before naptime).

Not only that, I didn't know what I was pledging allegiance for, I didn't know what I was pledging allegiance to, and I didn't even know what they meant by the word "America." What was this "America" we were all pledging ourselves to? I couldn't see it, or feel it, or touch it. It didn't make sense that the people around me, especially the adults, could get so roused about it. They played marching songs, gave long speeches, and talked about it as if it were something very special.

When I asked my parents and teachers about "America," they got all puffed up and told me how lucky I was to be living in this land we call "America." They said that it was the greatest place in the world because we were really free here, and the rest of the people around the world weren't as lucky as us.

I asked them why "America" was so special, and why the whole world wasn't as special as us, and they told me that there were bad people out there—people they called "our enemies."

They said that we "Americans" were freer than everyone else, and we stuck together and protected each other from "our enemies." It was implied that "our enemies" were my enemies too, and that just by being born here I would naturally agree with this idea about "our enemies."

Of course, nowadays I see all the suffering these pledges and allegiances have caused us, and I have rescinded the agreements I made when I was young. Those who know me know that I am not anti-American or anti-anything. Nor am I opposing any nation or anyone's right to identify and align with a country. I simply do not see the wisdom in continuing to separate ourselves into nations when it's so obvious that our Highest Good comes from knowing we are all children of the Earth. We are all members of the Human Family.

The Pledge of Alignment

I pledge alignment with the Highest Light on Earth and Heaven alike. And with its reflection, for which I stand, One Family, One with God, Indivisible, with liberty and blessings for all.

An Open Letter to Our Young Adults (and for Conscious Parents to Give to Their Children)

You don't have to go. You don't have to fight, kill anyone, be wounded, wound others, or die for your country. You don't have to be a walking target, which is what you surely become the minute you put on the uniform of a soldier. You don't have to take a chance on cutting your precious life short for reasons that were never made clear and never made sense.

Oh sure, you've been told that it is honorable and patriotic to serve your country, and that you are needed to defend your countrymen against enemies who are out to get you. But ask yourself, is this really true? Are there enemies who are out to get you, or are you being asked to do the bidding of a conglomerate of large profit-making corporations by attacking someone else who has never done one single thing wrong to you?

Let's face it: you've been lied to. From the time you were in kindergarten, you've been programmed to become a soldier, and to defend your fellow countrymen and women against all enemies. But who are those enemies? Are they the innocent civilians—men, women, and children—that your own country bombs and kills every day, or are they the fat-cat business people who manage the oil, manufacture the guns and bombs, maintain the military bases, and monetize the media that tells you what you're supposed to do on their behalf, lest they hunt you down and harm you too?

Who are your enemies? Are they the simple peasants working in their rice paddies or living in small desert villages who want only to be left alone to live out their lives without your interference? Or are they the ones who orchestrate it all? Are they the ones who spark the war by telling you who your enemies are supposed to be?

Do not let yourself be fooled for another minute. Every conflict in recent times has been deliberately created by those who would profit from it. From the sinking of the Lusitania in World War I, to the bombing of Pearl Harbor in World War II, to the Gulf of Tonkin ruse in Viet Nam, to the attacks on 9/11 that led America into Afghanistan and then Iraq to hunt for the (finally acknowledged) nonexistent weapons of mass destruction, all of these have been plotted and planned out in corporate boardrooms by men who wear coats and ties and who will never experience the horrors of battle for themselves.

They care not if you live or die, or even worse, if you step on a landmine and have to live out the rest of your days as an amputee. They care only about their money and how they can make more of it.

It is pure fact that most of the young men and women who sign up for military service wish they'd never done it, especially once they set foot on foreign soil. Most of them would give anything to go back home, take an honest, fulfilling job, and be with their loved ones. Most long for a life of happiness and opportunity, far away from a battlefield where they run the risk of being killed at any moment.

I urge you to take a closer look at the strange idea that keeps all these war wheels in motion: that we are protecting our fellow countrymen and our way of life by going over there and fighting; that we are making things safer and better for our families here at home by being an aggressor in someone else's land. In truth, we are actually doing just the opposite. Think about this long enough to get as clear as you can on it. By being an aggressor in someone else's land we make them hate us, and we cause them to think about attacking us back. In other words, by attacking others preemptively, we invite an attack upon ourselves. Is this how we are supposed to be keeping our country safe for our present and future generations? No. When you really begin to see through all of the smokescreens, you can't help but understand that attacking another will never keep your homeland safe or your freedom alive; it will only dig you deeper into the hellhole of war.

So, let's go back to where we started. You don't have to go. If you truly love your life, if you truly think about it and can't come up with one good reason why you should go to someone else's country and kill them, if you truly want, from this moment forward, to live in peace, to have a family of your own someday, to help your fellow men and women, no matter where they live, to work at a job you love, to know that you did something for the good of all humanity, and, instead of taking a chance on cutting your precious life short, to go into your old age having lived your life to the fullest with a clear conscience, knowing you have never deliberately brought suffering or death to another, then—before you make any agreements with the military, agreements you'll likely wish you hadn't made—please, please reconsider.

Take your chances out in the great unknown. Hide for a while if you have to. Learn to get the things you need to come to you by intending them into your life. Drop out, be a gypsy, become a minister, or live on the fringes of the world for a time. Anything is better than being a soldier.

The Amazing Frequency Freak Show

I have a good friend in the Caribbean who is having all sorts of challenges. Normally she is a strong, happy, and productive student as she goes about her days living in a beautiful tropical environment. But over the last several months she's been fatigued, confused, and sad. She has gone to the doctors and they have run many tests, but they can't find any specific cause for her physical or emotional conditions.

She wants a happy life, but her whole family, including her aging parents, is dealing with various health challenges of their own, and she has to take care of them. Now she's caught up in a cycle where she is sick and having to care for her sick family at the same time, and her dreams of returning to the university and doing what she loves to do are quickly disappearing. Her outlook on life, which was once so sparkly and spirited, has turned to despair. We Intenders are working to help her raise her energy level to the point where she can no longer be touched by outside influences, but there is clearly something interfering, something we haven't seen . . .

The Amazing Frequency Freak Show is so insidious, so touchy, that it is hard for anyone who truly cares about the quality of life and the goodwill of all men and women to talk about. The frequencies of our bodies as well as the frequencies of the places we live and visit are being messed with. The key intersections of the Earth's magnetic grid (the ley lines and vortices) have been taken over for the purpose of blasting dissonant frequencies at the people. We are being experimented on, and if you don't believe it, go outside and take a look at the tops of the mountains and hills around your city. They're filled with towers of all kinds.

Likewise, the military operates several huge transmitters in remote places capable of affecting large areas of the population. Our entire Earth is being covered with towers. Cell phone calls aren't the only things on the airwaves. What are they transmitting?

It is well known that in the nineteen-forties and fifties the Russians were experimenting with frequencies and targeting them at specific places. One of those places was the American Embassy.

They set the frequency for a low pulsating drone designed to disorient anyone in its range and they transmitted it only on certain days. On the days when the transmitter was turned on, the Americans complained of headaches, confusion, anger, weakness, and a variety of uncomfortable conditions. The number of days off work due to sickness rose dramatically. If we could do that back then, can you imagine what we are capable of doing today?

Make no mistake: The most destructive weapons of these times are not bombs, guns, and armies. These things are only window dressings compared to the potential damage of invisible frequencies. The prime weapon today is frequency, and people are being manipulated, sickened, weakened, angered, and disoriented by technologies that boggle the mind, literally!

And now, in order to make sure that we never escape their clutches, the powers that be are preparing us for their last trick, their grand finale—the radio-frequency identification (RFID) chip. In suggesting it, they will make it sound like the greatest thing since the invention of the wheel, but nothing could be further from the truth. For once we allow ourselves to have the chip implanted in our bodies, we will no longer be able to buy anything, sell anything, or go anywhere without somebody else knowing about it. Even worse, the chip can be triggered to affect our individual frequency without affecting anyone else around us. Freedom as we know it would be lost forever—and all our children, and all future generations, would live their entire lives under the control of veiled masters they never see.

The RFID chip is already in our passports and driver's licenses in some states and it has been secretly implanted and tested under the guise of being a vaccine. It represents a direct assault upon our health, our sanity, our personal power, our privacy, and all aspects of our daily lives, and we must never allow it to happen. From this moment forward we must withhold our agreement from anyone who advocates such dark measures, and we must stand strong on behalf of our body's natural integrity, never permitting anyone to implant any substances or technologies into us that would impede our freedom.

Please know this: This is not a topic that is comfortable to write about, nor is it likely a topic that is uplifting for you. If this issue were not being forced upon us, I would never discuss it here. However, this book is about We the People gathering our personal power for ourselves, not gathering it for someone else to do with as they please just because they are more devious than we anticipated. It is about us reaching the pinnacle of human evolution, not cycling back into the depths of slavery.

This having been said, it is our intention that you see through this monstrous trick, and that you see the wisdom in being the one who chooses what you will or will not allow to be placed in your body. The RFID chip is permanent. Once it is implanted, you cannot easily remove it. Your freedom and all that you long for and live for is at stake. *May you have ears to hear.*

Nothing can touch you when you keep your energy level high.

CHAPTER 2

The Ties That Bind

Agreements come in all shapes and sizes. Some would bind us for a morning, and others for a lifetime. Likewise, some are benevolent and very helpful, and others are reminiscent of the man who is smiling real big and waving friendly-like at you with one hand, while his other hand is picking the wallet out of your pocket.

It is for us to discern whether a potential agreement offers the promise of a greater burden or more freedom. Indeed, our freedom is usually, though not always, a good litmus test for deciding whether to make an agreement or not. The fact is that we never need to make an agreement. Not one is required. The great masters who walk this Earth withhold their agreement and remain free more often than not.

Of course, this idea is a little far-fetched in today's fast-paced world when we consider that the opportunities to make agreements are literally all around us. Nevertheless, it seems that the people who have the most freedom are the ones with the fewest agreements. They don't have to get to work on time, meet you for lunch, like your looks, wash your car, fight your wars, put the check in the mail, etc. They know that their yesses and their nos are always equally available, and they don't hesitate to use their no to remain less obligated and freer to do what they want to do.

Making wise use of the Law of Agreement will bring you more freedom right away. That having been said, let's have a look at a few different kinds of agreements so we'll be ready for them when they come our way.

Commiseration Agreements

Commiseration is a particularly enticing kind of agreement that is so subtle that we can be up to our neck in it before we realize what's happening. You know how it goes: someone starts complaining about something, and, like the bobble-head doll on the dashboard, you find yourself nodding and agreeing with them—and perhaps even telling a story about how you've had some of the same sort of problems they're talking about. On the surface it seems harmless enough, but underlying it all is the reinforcement of situations that really don't do anybody any good. It's just another way we sabotage ourselves.

Oftentimes, when people are looking for someone to commiserate with them, they have a vested interest in their suffering. They don't really want to change, or they're seeking validation for their problems; they're looking to keep things the way they are, instead of getting better. They want to continue to receive the money, the medicines, the perks, or the attention that they've become accustomed to receiving.

That's how we can tell the difference between commiseration and compassion. The person who evokes your compassion is truly suffering and looking for a way out of it.

The person who wants you to commiserate with them is usually protecting the status quo. To discern which is which, check in with your feelings. Compassion elicits a feeling of love and empathy toward the sufferer, while commiseration leaves you feeling down and asking yourself why you felt you had to add to another's problems (and your own) by agreeing with them.

I was having coffee with my buddy Jason, and before we even got into how we were going to approach our day's work, he started grumbling about how money was short, the customers didn't appreciate him, and his back hurt all the time. Then he went into a rant about doctors and how they put pins into his back ten years ago. Before I knew it, I was telling him about my own history of back problems. I started describing how my injury occurred—and then I caught myself and stopped in midsentence . . .

Knowing that my thoughts and my words are creating my future, why would I want to be agreeing with him around a subject that was apt to bring both of us more pain? It made no sense. If my intention is to be in agreement with him, wouldn't it be better to rally around a subject that is more positive and productive? Wouldn't it be better to dwell on things that are apt to bring us more happiness, comfort, peace, or abundance?

From that moment on, I've stayed more alert and aware to what I'm saying. And anytime Jason goes back into his stance of wanting me to commiserate with him, I switch the subject to something more positive. I'm not sure how long it will take him to catch on, but I began to feel better the minute I stopped commiserating.

If a friend of yours is telling you how sick they are and everything that's wrong with them, always remember to see them in their perfection. If you add to their illness by your belief in it, you are not doing them any good.

Contractual Agreements

Envision, for a moment, what occurs when you first make a contractual agreement. Usually one of two things happens: either you feel good and you're excited about the opportunities the agreement represents, or you're less than tickled and you feel a sense of trepidation over having signed the contract. In the first instance, you naturally feel free to move forward, as it shows all the signs of being a win-win situation. Typically, you place a measure of trust in the project or relationship and take it a step further.

In fact, there is a guideline that will help us in discerning before we make contracts or agreements with someone else. Anyone who is dedicated to making a win-win agreement will be willing to call off the agreement whenever you want to. That's how you know you're in a win-win situation—the person will treat you the way you want to be treated; they will respect your wishes. In fact, when people and institutions really love one another, there will be no need for contracts. Each would be willing to let the other go free at any moment.

If you change your mind or are unable to be responsible for an agreement you've made, it's best to let the other person know as soon as possible.

In the second instance, however—the one where you are feeling fearful or uncomfortable about it—it is wise to stop and take a good look before signing on the dotted line. Think things through and feel it through. Most often, in these types of win-lose situations, you'll see that there is some kind of threat involved. It will be something like: *If you don't make this agreement, something bad will happen to you.* The other person or institution is presenting you with uncomfortable scenarios which may place you in jeopardy, and it will seem like the only way out of your discomfort is to go along with them and make the agreement.

These potential win-lose or lose-lose agreements are the ones to watch out for, and they are prevalent all over our world today. You know how they work: *if you don't buy this car, you won't be able to get to work and support yourself; if you don't join the army, we won't be able to withstand an attack from outside invaders, and your freedom will be in danger; if you don't take this pill, your body will fall apart; if you don't buy this insurance policy, you won't be protected,* and so on.

As you can see, all of these examples start with the suggestion, *"If you don't . . ."* This is how fear works. The other person or institution, in order to get you to do what they want, preys upon your vulnerability and presents you with a worst-case, loss-oriented scenario. They literally plant a seed in your mind of a negative outcome—an outcome that can only be avoided if you do what they say. And if, perchance, you don't sign their contract or go along with them, they'll try to scare you even further. In the life insurance industry, they teach this tactic to their new sales reps; they even give it a name, calling it "backing the hearse up to the door," and it represents the lowest form of coercion.

Again, these are the kinds of suggestions we need to be alert for, because they can only sap our energy and bring us pain in the long run. In terms of the way our thoughts work, they cause us to envision, and thus create, situations and experiences that we really wouldn't have wanted to create for ourselves. The seeds of suffering came into our lives only because they were planted there by someone else.

This is the place where we must always remind ourselves that our thoughts are creating our world, and there are certain thoughts we might be entertaining that won't give us the results we're looking for. Then we must have the courage to say no to any proposed negative suggestions and trust that everything will turn out fine if we hold our thoughts only on our initial intended outcomes.

From this point on, we can breathe a big sigh of relief because we didn't fall for a win-lose agreement that would have encumbered us, potentially for years of our life. Instead, we remembered that the Laws of Manifestation always work, and we trusted in the innate goodness of the Universe to care for those who stay awake to what they are thinking and feeling.

You cannot be seduced without your consent.

Conscious Agreements

My first mentor B.J. used to talk a lot about agreement. According to him, the art of communication involved taking a thought that's in your head and placing it in someone else's head—and to do that, you have to get into agreement with them, at least for a while.

"Most folks don't have the slightest idea of what it takes to communicate," he said one day as we pounded nails into the deck we were building on the side of my small coffee shack. "They chatter about this and that, but they aren't committed to passing along any knowledge or information that would really help the other person."

"I'm not sure I follow you," I said.

"That's because you were never taught how to communicate. You were only taught how to talk."

Ouch.

"Real communication—that is, giving away information and knowing that it's been appropriately received by the other person so that a change in their Being occurs—may take many years. It isn't something you generally do over coffee and bagels. There is a process, and first you have to get along with the other person; you have to get into agreement with them or else they'll bolt right away.

"Think back to when we first met," he said. "We played music together at a party down the road, and I was playing songs that you liked. I was getting into agreement with you."

I remembered the Robinsons' party at the end of Rabbit Hill Road where we sang "Me and Bobby McGee" at the top of our lungs. The whole roomful of people joined in with us.

"You didn't have an inkling of what was going on. From your point of view, we were having fun—and that's true, we were. But from my point of view, I was also getting into agreement with you so that later on I would be in a position to pass this great body of esoteric information on to you. If I hadn't

hung out with you and talked about the things that fascinated you, worked side by side with you on the farm projects that interested you so much, or played the songs you liked on the guitar, we'd likely have never gotten together in the first place."

I thought about that conversation for a long time. B.J. and I were the best of friends for over seventeen years. During the seventies and eighties we maintained our isolated mystery school in the dense rainforest of Kona, Hawaii and, looking back, I could clearly recall times when he used agreement to keep me interested in what he was saying.

It was only after many years that I figured out what was going on. He was conscious and doing his best to bring me to consciousness, and I was asleep and being played by anyone who wanted something from me and was using agreement to get it. From that point on, I looked at everyone differently. I became interested in their true motives, and I had to learn to discern who had my best interests at heart and who didn't. Like B.J. often said, "Tony, there are some folks I watch, and some folks I watch out for."

I remember him saying that like it was yesterday—mainly because of what he said next. "It's true, Tony. Most folks don't communicate. They talk because they want something from you, and they typically want it right away. They're not committed to you having an experience of understanding or gaining any new knowledge that would further you along your path. They only want what they want, and they unconsciously use their agreement to get it."

I was lost in thought, and he pulled me back by looking me straight in the eyes. "Yeah, they're only in it for the short run. They don't have the consciousness or the patience it takes to pass along anything of real value to you. You and I, on the other hand . . . we made an agreement of a different sort. You don't remember it, but we made an agreement long ago, when we were in our souls, before we ever came down here to occupy these wondrous physical bodies on this amazing planet. We agreed that I would communicate this body of information to you until you got it. We didn't concern ourselves with how long it would take. However long it took would be however long it took—and if it took us several lifetimes, give or take a few, that was okay with us."

I haven't seen B.J. in a long time. We parted company several years ago but I know he'll show up when I'm ready for the next phase of our agreement. Until then, I'm reminded of something else he told me as we were saying our goodbyes. He said, "Tony, you don't have it until you can give it away." With that in mind, I give these stories to you, my gracious reader, so that you and I can both be moving forward and taking our next step in life.

Some of our agreements stay with us across time and space, from lifetime to lifetime. We carry them in our soul.

Rescinding Agreements

Letting go of an agreement always makes us freer. On a subtle but very real level, every agreement we make ties us to something or someone, and it is in letting go of the agreement that the ties are broken. Of course, while the ties and threads are serving us, we may want to keep them intact. However, many ties and relationships are encumbering, and it is wise for us to reevaluate them.

Here is a list of common agreements most of us have made throughout our lives that we may want to reconsider.

1. I need to work hard to get what I want.
2. I can really own things.
3. I'll be happier if I have a lot of money.
4. The media has my best interests at heart.
5. My teachers in school know more than me.
6. It's good to be patriotic.
7. My country is worth more to me than my life.
8. Fighting will give me the results I'm looking for.
9. Everything that comes to me is good for me.
10. This is the only world there is.
11. Fearing God makes good sense.
12. Religion and Spirituality are the same thing.
13. When I die, it's all over.
14. The doctors know best.
15. Times are hard.
16. It's okay if I'm being monitored or watched.
17. It's good to go along with the crowd.

You will remember when you made some of these agreements, and, for others, you won't have a clue when you agreed to them. Fortunately, it doesn't matter if you remember exactly when you first made these agreements. What's important is that you begin to take a good look at them and reevaluate them in light of where you stand today. This list may be a little disconcerting for some, and I suggest that you look at it with a playful spirit. Have fun letting go of these old agreements—for with each one you let go of, your freedom increases.

Not only that, we can raise our consciousness by withdrawing our agreement. In fact, the Universe gives us opportunities every day to lift ourselves up and out of our encumbering agreements, and oftentimes all we have to do is learn to keep ourselves from nodding our head or saying okay or uh-huh.

Think about it for a moment. Every time someone else, whether it's a good friend in casual conversation or a TV newsperson, presents us with an idea or a belief, we are simultaneously being offered the chance to go along with them (and thus strengthen their belief), or to reject (or simply not react to) what they are saying. And in doing so, we refrain from tying ourselves to their encumbering ideas.

In this way, the world becomes our schoolroom, and our daily life provides all the lessons we need in order to grow. In the past we've gone along with just about everything people have suggested to us (we humans are very suggestible beings), but now, we're going to be more alert than ever to our own knee-jerk reactions and stop ourselves from nodding or stating our agreement. And here's the kicker: every time we refrain from reacting or nodding in any way, we will have just raised our consciousness, and everything in our life will proceed differently from that moment forward.

In each instance, we've become less suggestible, more discerning, and more empowered. Others will no longer have the ability to control us like they used to. And soon, perhaps when we least expect it, we'll come to a moment in our lives when we will have a wondrous new realization: that we are each our own person, able to stand tall within our own sovereignty and integrity. No one else rules us, because now we rule ourselves.

In the moment we change a habit pattern
we also raise our consciousness.

I've always enjoyed window-shopping. You know what window-shopping is: it's going out to the stores with no intention of buying anything. When I window-shop, I tell myself that today I'm leaving my wallet in my pocket. I'm just going to look in the windows, no matter how temptingly the shop owners have presented their wares.

I treat our current way of life the same way. I'm only window-shopping it. I'm not buying anything anymore. For instance, when the media tells me there is some new problem out there, and the solution is now being made available to everyone, I simply observe it. My experience has taught me time and time again that the media is self-serving, and they have no interest whatsoever in my well-being. In fact, it's just the opposite—the media creates problems in order to get us to buy their ideas and consumer goods.

In the old days, I would have gotten angry and begun to oppose their media hype, thus dissipating my precious energy. But now I just window-shop. I observe only—with no emotional attachment to the ideas they're selling on TV and in the newspapers. I'm not buying any of it, so it's no longer affecting me. This is one of the keys to our ultimate happiness.

We gain our freedom by becoming observers.

Tools for Discernment

Discernment is so important in these times, and it will be your greatest ally once you make friends with it. If you ever have to make a challenging decision about whether to agree with someone about an idea, you can take advantage of the tools used by many cultures in the past. Pendulums, dowsing rods, muscle testing, the I Ching, divination cards, and many other tools will help you to discern.

The most common method of applying these tools requires that you make a statement to yourself before you begin. The statement is: "It's in my highest and best good if I agree and go along with such and such an idea." If, for instance, the pendulum or muscle test gives you a Yes response, then you can feel free to move forward. However, if the pendulum gives you a No response, then you can withhold your agreement and not think about the idea anymore. Naturally, this means of discerning requires a measure of trust on your part. But after you practice with it, and your intuition blossoms, you will find that you can use it for all sorts of issues that arise in your life.

If you are interested in obtaining a pendulum for your personal use in discerning, you can go to my website at *www.intenders.com/tools.html.*

CHAPTER 3

The Law of Adversity

Adversity comes when we're getting something that we don't want, or we want something that we're not getting. Either way, life is not going exactly as we'd like it to go—or is it? What if, on a subconscious or a soul level, we set ourselves up to experience some adversity in one form or another? Sounds crazy, doesn't it? But when you think about it, it could be that maybe, just maybe, that's what we're doing. But why?

The Law of Adversity is the counterpart to the Law of Agreement, and it offers us many insights about our uncomfortable experiences. The Law of Adversity says that *along with every challenge or problem we encounter, an opportunity also presents itself.* It is important for us to be alert and aware so that we can spot these opportunities and turn them into gifts for ourselves. For this to happen, though, it helps if we realize that we made *an agreement* to be here at this time. We set it all up—all of the chaos, adversity, resistance, limitation, all of it—so that we could rise above it and reach our highest calling in life.

How else would we get stronger, unless we had challenges along the way to bring out the best in us? How else would we learn to treasure a peaceful life for ourselves, if we hadn't been through a conflict or two? How else would we conjure up courage, if we didn't have a few fears to rise above? We need our challenges. We agreed to deal with them so we could evolve to a higher, happier place.

I don't know about you but I'm being tested a lot nowadays. Recently, I was driving Highway 89A, the awe-inspiring narrow road that runs out of Flagstaff into Sedona, Arizona. I was on my way to Phoenix, where part of my soul family was gathering in preparation to take The Intenders Road Show out to the world. About halfway down the mountain, on the steep road that snakes through Oak Creek Canyon, my van started smelling weird, like something was burning. Since there was no place to pull over and no mechanic in sight, I decided to keep going—and I intended that I would make it to town safely.

By the time I reached Sedona, smoke was billowing out of the right front side of the hood. With the burning odor so strong I could hardly stand it, I coasted into the parking lot of a local health food store—just as my brakes gave out!

Parking behind an adobe wall, I got out to take a look and saw that my right front wheel had been on fire. Something inside (it turned out to be the rubber boot) was still smoldering. Now, I'm a bit of a mechanic, but without special tools and a few new parts, there was no way I could work on it—especially in a health food store parking lot. All I could do was intend that I find a good mechanic and also intend that he or she charged me less than the $800 I had to my name at the time.

Looking around and seeing only tourist shops, I decided to go into the health food store and find a phonebook to locate a mechanic or a tow truck. As I walked across the hot asphalt, a pretty lady who was having coffee on a patio nearby smiled and waved at me like we were old friends. I walked up, introduced myself, and told her of my plight. She said her name was Garielle and asked where my van was. I showed her, and she pointed to the adobe wall and said, "On the other side of that wall is the main street. And right across from us, behind those trees over there, is my friend's shop. His name is Karl, and he's the best mechanic in town."

Long story short, in less than two minutes we were in Karl's office; within thirty minutes, he had given me a quote of $600 to replace my front brakes, rotors, calipers, boots, and wheel bearings; and by the end of the day my van was working perfectly again and I was back on the road, heading for Phoenix with $200 still left in my pocket!

Not too long ago, I would have gotten flustered at this seemingly strange turn of events. But this time I didn't. I stayed on the bright side, made my intentions, and knew that it would all work out for the Highest Good. And you know what? It did! In fact, looking back on it all, I was filled with gratitude throughout the entire experience. I made several new friends, got to hang out in Sedona all day, and I eventually ended up living there for part of the winter. My van couldn't have broken down in a better place!

Be open for all opportunities, because sometimes they come in different packages than you are imagining.

Interruptions

Inertia is the natural tendency for something that is moving to keep moving and something at rest to keep resting. It plays a much larger part in our lives than we know. For one thing, inertia is the cause of most of the adversity we encounter. Now, inertia by itself won't spark any emotional charge. But when interruptions show up, adversity comes into play.

Think about it. You're going along, in the middle of something—it could be anything, from walking to the refrigerator to getting ready for an important business meeting—and you're interrupted. That's what inertia and adversity do when they come together. They cause interruptions that typically give rise to an emotional release, like anger or frustration.

Let's look at a couple of examples. The other day I was in a nice flow of events, getting ready to meet a friend for dinner. I was right on schedule, and all I had left to do was stop in the grocery store to pick up a couple of items for the salad. When I got to the store, it was packed. All of a sudden my nice flow of events—the inertia—was threatened. By the time I got to the checkout line, there were ten people ahead of me, and with each moment that passed, I got more frustrated. My flow had stopped. I was going to be late. By the time I made it to the head of the line, I was completely discombobulated. Sound familiar?

Here's another scenario on a different level. A friend of mine was in a wonderful relationship with a beautiful woman a few years ago. Everything was going along fine, they were deeply in love, and he thought they were going to spend the rest of their lives happily together. But one day, from out of the blue, something changed. An old boyfriend of hers came over for a visit. As the three of them sat there chatting, it became clear to my friend that she was obviously flirting with her old boyfriend. She couldn't keep her hands off of him. My friend had never seen her do anything like this before. There was no mistaking it—she did it several times right in front of him. And in that moment, he knew it was over for them.

This was a big-time interruption for my friend. He'd spent years with this woman, planning, traveling, loving, enjoying every moment—and now it was all gone because he couldn't trust her anymore. Can you imagine the depth of emotional charge he had to release? It was monumental in his life, and he had to deal with it.

B.J. used to say *"the symbols change, but the functions remain the same."* The symbols in these instances are very different: having to wait in a long line versus having to deal with a failed relationship. But the function for both is the same: the inertia was interrupted; the flow we were in came to an unexpected halt.

That's the way adversity usually works, and you don't have to think for very long to come up with tons of examples of how it has affected you in your own life. The function, again, is the same, but the symbols are many. For example, you may stub your toe, lose your job, break up with your mate, get foreclosed on, or have car troubles. You may feel ill, need a check that doesn't come in the mail, experience bad weather, see an increase in taxes, see the war getting worse, arrive at the store just after it's closed, experience the economy getting worse, deal with crazy neighbors, and on and on. It's all adversity, and it's all an interruption or a change from the flow we were in. The question is, how do we deal with it?

When inertia is interrupted, our emotional charge builds up, and it seeks an outlet. We are not supposed to be like flashlight batteries, which have a limited capacity and are not to be overfilled. That's what causes leaks and explosions. Instead, we're supposed to be like conductors of energy, meant to have energy come into us and flow out of us smoothly. The challenge for many of us is that we've got a vested interest in our inertia. We want things to keep going along the way they have been. When a change or interruption occurs, we tend to blow it instead of flow it. And that's the key, right there. *Nothing is adverse if we're accepting of it unconditionally.*

When we're able to accept each change as it comes to us, we're no longer storing up our emotional charge and setting ourselves up for an emotional outburst or explosion that can have far-reaching effects for us and all those around us. On the contrary, when we accept our interruptions, we are allowing the energetic charge to flow through us and our lives begin to operate on an even keel. We become stronger in our integrity to stand firm in the face of our interruptions, and something else happens, something wonderful. As we learn to accept our challenges and flow the energy that comes through us, we open the doors to our creativity. We reroute the energy that we previously would have leaked out in the form of anger and emotional explosions, and we use it to express ourselves creatively. We use it for our art, our calling in life.

That's how the Law of Adversity works, once you master it.

When I was younger, I used to be a "tough guy," until one particular situation I was involved in showed me, ever so clearly, the wisdom in becoming nonviolent. An experience I had over sixteen years ago—in fact, it precipitated our having started The Intenders—is a great example of the Law of Adversity in action. I had been living on my land in Hawaiian Acres for several years, and life was good. My small coffee shack was situated in the middle of a dense rainforest, so I had complete privacy and could be a hermit all I wanted. I could have easily lived out the rest of my life in the tropical Hawaiian jungle, but a couple of things happened to change all of that.

Within a very short period of time, the properties on both sides of me were sold to people who said that they would respect my privacy, but in reality they had no intention of doing so. From the first day that the new neighbor to the north moved in, my whole world changed. For a solid year, he ran a loud generator, pounded nails, sawed boards, and made more noise than any six people. What was once my quiet refuge in the rainforest was now gone entirely. Over time, I resigned myself to living with the constant noise—noise that I had moved to the jungle to get away from.

About a year and a half later, my new neighbor to the south, Jim, began developing his beautiful parcel of raw, virgin, forested land. Jim flew in one day from Oregon, hired a D-9 bulldozer operator, and started bulldozing the land from pin to pin. Since my home was located along our shared property line, the bulldozer came within a few feet of it. Overnight, I went from living in a totally private environment to being right out in the open where anyone could see into my house. I couldn't believe it!

Adding insult to injury, the dozer man Jim hired—he was a gigantic, overweight pit bull of a man—started the dozer up at first light every morning. This went on for two weeks, and everyone in the neighborhood was rattled by having to begin their day with what sounded like World War III going on down the road. The neighbor across the street, a Filipino man everybody called "Black" (I don't have the slightest idea what his real name was) was especially mad about the early morning dozer noise, but he only grumbled among the immediate neighbors and never directly to the pit bull.

During the third week of this craziness, I finally blew it. About ten in the morning Jim came strutting up my driveway, and I was so angry that I stepped right up and took a swing at him (I was still acting like a tough guy back then). He was bigger than me, but I didn't care. My quiet was gone; my house now sat out in the open for all to see; and all of the work I had done to create a peaceful sanctuary for myself was for naught.

As it turned out, Jim was a champion middle-weight wrestler, and before I knew it, he had my body folded up like a pretzel. I was pinned on the ground with my arm bent behind my back, feeling like it was going to snap at any second. In that instant, the tough guy inside of me gave up, and Jim ultimately let me go, only after I promised never to come near him again.

I stumbled away, shaking, spitting, and thinking about how foolish I had been. That would have been the end of the story, except that the very next day, as I walked down my driveway to water the gardens, the pit bull dozer guy came toward me with his immense belly hanging out from between his suspenders. I could see he was furious! As he got closer, I stopped in my tracks and started backing up.

"I'm going to kill you!" he yelled, and he kept on coming.

"What for?" I shouted back, adrenaline surging through every cell in my body.

"You slashed my tires!" He was snarling and spewing with every word.

"What tires?" I screamed, as I continued to back up. "I don't know anything about your tires! What are you talking about?"

"Liar!" He yelled it so loud I practically jumped out of my skin. "You slashed all four of my truck tires, and I'm gonna kill you!" And he started running toward me but stopped, out of breath, as soon as he saw that he couldn't catch me.

"I didn't do it! I swear! I didn't do it!"

"Yes, you did," he yelled. "You took a swing at Jim yesterday, and you slashed my tires this morning, and I'm gonna kill you for it!"

Now, at least I was starting to get the picture. He thought I slashed his tires because I was still angry about losing my privacy. He was partially right—I still hadn't gotten over my anger yet—but I didn't slash his tires. It wasn't until several years later that I found out that Black, the Filipino neighbor, had knifed his tires because he was fed up with the constant dawn-to-dark noise from the D-9.

Long story short, the pit bull dozer man stopped coming at me, and I stopped backing up. We just stood there, about thirty feet apart, with him threatening to kill me when he caught me, and me swearing that "I didn't do it!" After about ten minutes of this, he finally turned around—and I ran, as fast as I could, into the thickest part of the jungle where he couldn't follow me.

I ended up walking for miles, arriving just before dark at the home of my future girlfriend and fellow Intenders cofounder, Betsy Palmer. Using the phone, I called my Kahuna buddy, Gary, and told him the whole story. All Gary said was that he would take care of it. He instructed me not to go home for a couple of days, but that everything would be fine after that. I asked him how he planned on resolving it all, but he just chuckled and said that he had his ways.

Three days later, per Gary's instructions, I went back home. The dozer was gone; the property next door was cleared in total; and Jim had flown back to Oregon. I never saw the pit bull man again, and I never figured out what Gary did to get rid of him. The Kahunas had amazing powers, of that I was positive. I had often heard stories about them, and now I had seen it for myself.

I was home at last, but it didn't feel the same after that. A couple of weeks later, I moved out of my beloved jungle house and moved in with Betsy—and within a month we held our first Intenders Circle. The Universe had set it all up so I would have to leave my home in the rainforest in order to step into my highest destiny. From that point on, I knew I was aligned with my life's calling and armed with a new mantra, which eventually became the basis for the first line of The Code: "I refrain from opposing or harming anyone." It just never made sense to think about deliberately harming anyone else after having lived through those strange experiences in Hawaiian Acres. After all, you never know when the tough guy inside of you will run into a pit bull or a wrestling champion down the road.

Oftentimes the changes that you are forced to go through are put there so you will remember what it is like to be at the crest of the hill and excited about what's on the other side. It's about getting out of your Continuous Comfort Zone.

Our Continuous Comfort Zone

Our Continuous Comfort Zone (CCZ) will keep us from fulfilling the calling we set for ourselves long, long ago. You see, all of us have projects that we arranged and agreed to do here on Earth, and if we stay in our CCZ too long, we won't be as apt to do the things we came here to do. Accordingly, the Highest Good will see to it that we are removed from places, relationships, and situations so that we can have something better. The challenge with this is that we tend to think we want to stay where we are; we're not always able to see around the corner to a time when things will be better because we left the place we were in. So the Universe will begin to make the places or relationships we're in go stale or become uncomfortable.

Tina Stober, my other fellow Intenders cofounder, and I have had this happen so many times that we've given a name to it. We call it "getting kicked out" of our CCZ. The Universe literally sees to it that we can't go back where we were; all of a sudden, everything that was extremely comfortable up to this point in our lives becomes so topsy-turvy and threatening that we have to look elsewhere for our next step in life.

As for me, I am certain that I never would have left my farms in Hawaii, started The Intenders community, or written *The Code* if the Universe hadn't come along and upset my entire world. In each instance I was deeply ensconced in places and relationships that were so pleasant that I never would have moved had the circumstances around me not changed drastically.

In Kona, I spent eighteen amazing years on one of the most beautiful farms you've ever seen. B.J. and I owned it

together. He was passing a wondrous body of esoteric information along to me on a daily basis, the fruit was dripping
off of the trees, life was as good as it gets. Then one day, B.J.
announced that I had learned all that he could teach me in
this environment. It was time for me to go out into the world
and put the information I had learned to the test. Of course,
I squawked. I told him there was no way I was ever going to
leave my home. No way. Period. I had worked too hard to
get it the way it was. And besides that, I loved it as much as
anyone could love anything.

Then several strange things occurred all at once. The trade
wind patterns shifted, and the vog—the sulphuric smoke from
Kilauea Volcano—blew into Kona. A smelly cloud settled into
the bowl that outlined the mountain ridge all the way from
Holualoa to South Point. What was once one of the most magnificent, untouched spots on the Earth was now a toxic mess.

At the same time, the local large landowners of the Big
Island began to enforce the laws regarding the number of
houses people could have on their lands. Back in the eighties,
before Kona became a major retirement destination, there
were so many acres of empty rainforest and so few residents
that people regularly walked into the jungle and put up a coffee shack. Everybody knew it, and nobody cared. Now, almost
overnight, all that changed.

B.J. and I each had our own small coffee shack on our four
and a half acres, and according to the local politicos, one of us
would have to tear his house down and leave. Long story short,
after a lot of angry words, a standoff during which B.J. and I
were each ready to tear the other apart (he was much bigger
than me), and a friendship of eighteen years gone sour, I left. I
saw him only once after that, but I can tell you this: he knew.

He knew I had a calling to write books and create a one-of-a-kind community, and that I would never have written the first word if I had stayed on the farm.

Eight years later, I was happily entrenched on my three-acre parcel of land outside of Hilo when a similar situation with the pit bull dozer operator occurred. As I said earlier, it is highly unlikely that I would have gone to Betsy's place, nor would we have started up The Intenders, if the Universe hadn't taken my home away from me. It seems like the Law of Adversity was working overtime on my behalf, though I didn't know it at the time. I didn't want to leave Hawaiian Acres, but, looking back, I'm sure glad I did.

The same thing happened again around the turn of the century in New Mexico. I'd manifested a life of complete and total abundance for myself there for several years. I was living on a horse ranch outside of Albuquerque when my girlfriend's cousin came to visit. He was acting weird, so she and I got into an argument about him. Her cousin was a much larger, mysterious kind of a guy, and he stepped in and began screaming and choking me—and she didn't stop him! Long story short again, within hours (after all sorts of threats and police reports), I was on the road, down to my last dime, and not knowing where to go.

I spent the night with my friend, Sandy Mathers, and drove west to California the next morning. Shortly after that I took a walk along Grover Beach on the Central California coast and I heard a voice in my head say, "Support Life—I refrain from opposing or harming anyone. I allow others to have their own experiences . . ." and The Code: 10 Intentions for a Better World was born. As I mentioned earlier, I seriously doubt that I would have written The Code had I stayed in *the comfort of the ranch in Albuquerque. Once again, the Universe knew better for me than I knew for myself.*

These are not the times to allow ourselves to get too attached to our CCZs. The world is changing so fast that we must be ready to flow and to go where we are most needed. We each have amazing, life-changing experiences awaiting us; however, we cannot expect to avail ourselves of these gifts as long as we stay stuck in our CCZs.

The Law of Adversity sends us some strange paradoxes. Many of us have worked our whole lives in order to put ourselves in a position to live out our dream in comfort and relative peace. But now, what with the shifting of the ages, there is a gem being offered in the form of a whole new way of life. This gem shines with the promise of a new day where all of us—each and every man, woman, and child—are lifted up into a true comfort zone: a comfort zone that isn't built upon a foundation of human scarcity and suffering, but a permanent comfort zone that is predicated and firmly anchored in love and peace for all, for all time.

When things begin to break or go sour something better is on its way to you.

CHAPTER 4

Community:
The Together Agreement

In The Intenders we have said all along that there are two things we must do if we're going to make a difference in our lives and in the lives of everyone around us. The first is to get proficient at manifesting, because until we are able to use the Laws of Manifestation to get what we want to come to us, we remain pawns in someone else's game.

The second "difference maker" reminds us that if we're going to manifest a better world for ourselves—a world where we live in peace, joy, comfort, freedom, grace, and abundance—then we must begin to come together in community. Our present-day system, where we've been divided, separated, and isolated into countless factions, is barely serving us. Now is the time for us to begin to see the wisdom and to reap the huge rewards that come from working together for the Highest Good of the whole.

Being part of a community doesn't mean that everybody is necessarily going to live together.

Last year, I was sitting in Healing Haven Bookstore (now The Alabaster Jar) in Astoria, Oregon chatting with my good friend, Jane Holland, and her friend Amber, a fiery lady with a bit of sadness in her brow. We were talking about the advantages of working together in community, and then Amber told us this story.

A few months back, my whole world was upside down. My husband had just passed away, I was working at a dead-end job, my bills were piling up, and to top it all off, the county had started dumping some sort of nasty toxic waste in my backyard. It smelled horrible and made both me and my animals sick. I didn't know what to do.

One night shortly after my husband passed, I had a very vivid dream. My Spirit Guide, a Native American Medicine Woman, came and sat down before me. I began telling her all my problems, one at a time, and with every problem I mentioned, she said the same thing: "You can't do it!" When I said I was lonely and needed to get out and socialize, she said, "You can't do it!" When I said I needed more money to pay all the doctor's bills, she said, "You can't do it!" When I said I needed to move to get away from the toxic waste being dumped nearby, again, she said, "You can't do it!"

As you can imagine, I was getting very flustered, and as I began to express my frustration with her and all her "You can't do it!"s, she stopped me in the middle of my ranting and said, "You're not listening to me, Amber! You keep interrupting before I can finish my sentence. What I am trying to tell you is, 'You can't do it alone!'"

Two evenings later, I was invited to a drumming circle. They put chairs in the center of the circle while they called in the ancestors, drummed, and prayed for the healing of those sitting in the chairs. It was the first time I had ever gone to a true spiritual circle, and I haven't been the same since. Sitting in the circle that night with all my new friends showering me with their love, light, and support made me feel better than I'd felt in years. My cares and worries were lifted up and away as the old Medicine Woman's words came true. From that point on, I knew that I couldn't—and wouldn't—have to do it alone.

The Magical Flow

The first time I experienced the magic of working together, B.J. and I were building a rock wall together. We'd just hired our friend Toshi to bulldoze a new driveway on our property, and when he was finished, the lower side of the road needed to have a retaining wall constructed to keep the Kona afternoon rains from washing away the dozer work. There were plenty of large rocks strewn about the land and, since they were free, we decided to use them to build the wall.

When we began, B.J. showed me how to dig a flat footing—which was about forty feet long—put up the batter boards, and set the strings so the wall would be straight. At the time, it looked to me like it would take weeks to complete the job.

With the preliminary work accomplished, he started placing the rocks with the flattest side of each one facing outward and leaning ever so slightly into the hillside. My job, since I was new at this, was to gather the best rocks and have them ready for B.J. to set in line. At first, the job crept along very slowly. My work skills at that time were minimal, to say the least, primarily because I had been a college boy who'd never really done *any hands-on labor. As a result, B.J. spent a lot of time idle, waiting for me to bring him the rocks he needed.*

After about an hour of painstaking labor, we took a break and sat with our backs against the first few stones he'd set into place. The view of the entire southern Kona coast spread before us like a picture of paradise. B.J. wasn't enjoying it, though. He was staring at me with a disapproving scowl on his face.

"Didn't anyone ever show you how to work with someone else?" he asked me.

"No."

"Well," he said, "if we keep up our present pace, we'll be here all summer, building this wall. You've got to wake up!"

B.J. could be very direct at times. I'd learned not to take everything he said personally, but sometimes it was hard. He knew how to push my buttons, and when he initially introduced me to a body of knowledge he called The Information, I allowed him to test me so I could see my weaknesses and eventually be free of all my buttons. Little did I realize when I made that agreement, B.J. was a master at button-pushing. More than a few times, I'd end up walking away from a heavy conversation with him, muttering and cussing about how he could be such a jerk to insult me like he did.

I was just about ready to split this time, too, when he caught me. Now he spoke in a gentler, softer tone of voice. "One of the biggest problems in America today," he said, "is that people don't really know how to work together. We've got all sorts of fancy, highfalutin educational systems and we soak up tons of knowledge, but very few are able to put it to good use."

I listened because I needed the rock wall built. But my ego, which was puffed up by the fact that I had a college degree, wanted to scream in reaction.

"People are too isolated from one another nowadays," he went on. "They work by themselves, often in tiny cubicles, and never discover the joy that can come from working as part of a team. They never get to step into the magical flow which comes when two or more people are concentrated on a common project."

Now we're getting somewhere, I thought to myself. The magical flow sounded interesting.

"There's a coming together—a Oneness—that can occur whenever two people are working together and putting their attention on the same thing," he said. "It doesn't matter if they're in an office, on an assembly line, or working in a tool and die shop. In our case, it can happen right out here in the middle of the rainforest, while we're building this rock wall. But, we'd have to take extra care and keep an eye on what the other one is doing at all times."

"I can do that," I said, glibly.

"Well, up until now, you haven't," he responded. "If we're going to have any hope of stepping into the magical flow working together, you'll have to pay much closer attention to what I'm doing and make sure you have the next rock ready for me when I need it. Otherwise, I'll be sitting around, twiddling my thumbs, while you're off in the woods somewhere doing God knows what!"

The directness had returned, but direct or not, I knew he was right. And besides that, my interest was piqued. I wanted to check out the magical flow. So, from that point on, not only did I gather rocks, I watched what he was doing at the same time. It involved me having to do two things at once, but with a little practice I found that I was able to have the perfect rock sitting there for him so he didn't have to move more than six inches to pick it up and put it in the wall.

By the time we took our next break, the sun was high over-head and several hours had passed without me even noticing. I'd been so focused on the project at hand that it was like the rest of the world had gone away. I had never worked so hard and felt so good! I'd experienced a state of Oneness, as sweet as any I'd ever had in my meditations or prayers. And to top it all off, when I looked around me, there was fifteen feet of wall, five feet high, already backfilled and standing at the end of the day. A whole lot of work had gotten done while we were in the magical flow.

It all gets better when we work together.

Communities Who Really Care

Great things happen when people come together and agree to work on behalf of the highest interests for all concerned. In fact, the entire group prospers when the Highest Good of the whole and all of its members is taken into consideration. It's ironic that we are even discussing this bit of common-sense information, but unfortunately, it has been forgotten in recent times. So often nowadays we've allowed ourselves to be pushed around by big business or insensitive govern-ment. In fact, this has become so commonplace that it is a thing of great beauty when the people rescind their unserv-ing agreements and take their power back.

Several years ago my friend Cathy and I decided to take off on the back roads of Bali on our motor scooters and found our-selves in a small, forested, up-country village outside of Ubud. We were visiting with some of the locals while we sipped sodas and sweated from the intense heat when one of the villagers, an old man with a huge, welcoming smile, took a liking to us and started telling us a story.

He explained that all the townspeople of the small villages and towns of Bali had their own artistic specialty: some were predominately silversmiths, some worked with fabrics and made beautiful batiks, some painted detailed scenes of Bali life, and some were known for their fine woodcarvings.

The old man gestured gracefully with his hands as he told us that his village took great pride in carving the bright colored fish that Bali is so famous for. They had been fish carvers for many generations, keeping with the old ways of their ancestors by sawing the fallen trees with a large two-man bow saw. In this way they would cut the tree into thin slices and then take the slices to the artists who carved them into beautiful fish. It was a laborious task, but they were happy people and they liked doing it that way.

One day, one of his neighbors down the road bought a chain saw and started slicing the trees with it. Everything changed overnight! The neighbor was instantly producing fish slices a hundred times faster than everyone else in the village. Right away, a few other neighbors saw what was happening and they bought chain saws, too.

According to our new friend, the chain saw carvers produced so many fish so fast that they were able to drop their prices and they cornered the market, practically driving the old-timers out of business. Not only that, the quality of life in the village changed dramatically because of the noise factor. What had once been a quiet, peaceful place to live was now loud with the buzzing of chain saws all day long.

As things got worse, the elders of the village, who were chosen to act on behalf of the village as a whole, called a meeting.

After listening to everyone's points of view, it was decided that the use of chain saws was not good for the village.

The old man's eyes opened wider as he finished his story. When the elders made their proclamation, no one said a word in disagreement. The neighbors who were using the chain saws were quite happy to respect the goodwill of everyone in the village, and they put their chain saws away immediately. The peace and quiet of village life returned, and the markets stabilized within days because the Balinese villagers knew something that the rest of us had forgotten. They knew that everything worked best when the Highest Good of the whole community was honored.

As we move into a new paradigm, stories like this one are becoming more and more prevalent. Four states and several large U.S. cities have now outlawed the use of traffic-light cameras. The people don't want them and have had the gumption to stand up and voice their disagreement by voting the cams down. In my hometown of Pagosa Springs, Colorado, the people voted to remove the fluoride from the municipal water supply. It was a struggle, but we did it because we had proven, beyond any doubt, that it was harmful to our health.

People are speaking out now in great numbers because the days of the tyrants are going away and are being replaced by solutions that honor the Highest Good of all—not just the supposed good of the few in power. Indeed, a new day is dawning where the welfare, the beneficence, the health, the comfort, and the blessings of the people are being taken into consideration. The days are coming when we will enjoy the best that life has to offer, and in the meantime, We the

People must take heart and keep moving forward. Because it is up to us, not our leaders, to bring forth the new world.

If everyone is living the life they are here to live, and everyone is totally happy with their life and their families and their relationships and their work, can you imagine what that would be like?

The Family of One

Life keeps offering us the next thing. It's our choice whether we take it—whether we recognize our opportunities and make the most of them—or whether we let it go, nestle back into our Continuous Comfort Zone, and wait for another gift to come along. The key to our greatest happiness in life often lies in our alertness. Do we stay so focused on our latest drama, our favorite thoughts, our current distractions, that we let things slide by—or can we ratchet our alertness up a notch and take advantage of the gifts being offered?

All intentions, once manifested, end with a feeling—a feeling of satisfaction, joy, expansion. That expansion will lead us to our next step in life.

The times we're living in call for us to do some ratcheting. Everyone nowadays is being tested in one way or another. Clearly, there is so much testing going on that we can't ignore it or avoid it. The issue is not so much how we react to our tests; it's where these tests are leading us.

For those who are lining themselves up with the Highest Good, the tests lead to greatness and all that we have longed for. All we have to do to pass our tests is to be clear about the end result. Will it give us the outcome we're looking for? Does the end result feel good? It is a great truth that all intentions, once manifested, end with a feeling—a feeling of satisfaction, a feeling of joy, a feeling of expansion. And that expansion will then lead us to our next step in life.

For humanity, our next step is the Family of One. The Family of One starts with us coming together in our respective circles and communities so that each person can support everyone else in bringing the intentions, visions, and dreams of the whole—as well as the individual—to life. These intentions, visions, and dreams can vary from community to community. That is, it doesn't matter what those dreams and intentions are, as long as you are all willing to stand for the Highest Good. You could be intending to build a house, win a race, clean up a neighborhood, make uplifting music, or keep each other awake to your spiritual essence. Regardless of the nature of the project, the idea is to create a healthy environment where a state of Oneness is felt by everyone in the community.

I have experienced this kind of supportive setting so many times that it merits further discussion because it is so powerful. Like I said, something very special occurs when a group of people—it doesn't matter how many—get together and consciously agree to support each other in the manifestation of their intentions. Of course, in many instances it may not be wise to share your innermost intentions with others—especially those you hardly know. But when everyone in the group has a playful, lighthearted attitude and is willing to say that they align with you as well as with the Highest Good, then the door is opened for miracles to take place. We see this happen all the time in our Intenders Circles where people agree/align with others' intentions. Their intentions oftentimes manifest so fast it makes our heads spin.

Indeed, the purpose of these Circles is to provide a safe, encouraging environment where people can come together and consciously help each other to become more proficient at getting the things they want in their lives. When we expand this concept to include larger and larger circles of people, our agreement can make a huge difference in the way we live—and this is how the changes so many of us seek will ultimately come about in our world. As the groups who are in agreement with bringing forth a new way of life become larger, a groundswell of momentum builds and a new way of life appears.

As I write this, we are seeing this happen in our Intenders of the Highest Good Founders Circle on Facebook. Here is what Intender Carol Joy Bennett said about it in a recent post.

Our group just made another upward shift collectively! Gratitude, intend, agreement, gratitude, manifest, momentum, gratitude . . . I am grateful for momentum, the energy of movement. I love experiencing how others joining in agreement boosts my intent and assists me with greater momentum for manifesting and for discovering more desires to intend. I appreciate the feeling of being in the center of my flow of prosperity in every area of my life with likeminded people. It is a joyous party as we share our intents and manifest together. When we join in gratitude for this flow of goodness, we create a momentum for each other, just as if we were raising beautiful sails so we can sail higher into the atmosphere of the highest good together. I am grateful for momentum.

The Family of One is gaining momentum every day even though we may not hear anything about it in the mainstream media. The Family of One. *Think about it.* And when you do, doesn't it resonate? Doesn't the Family of One touch a chord deep within you? Doesn't it offer the promise of a better day, a day when you can walk the land openly without borders and false boundary lines, a day when you look freely into the eyes of anyone who comes your way, a day when you breathe easy because there is no longer anyone out to get you? Isn't the Family of One just as easy to believe in (and thus create for ourselves) as the jaded offerings from the media?

That's where our alertness comes in; that's where our opportunities are to be found. We can go along with the crowd and continue to keep our attention on the media matrix and all it stands for—or we can change. We can stay alert and accept the gift in our tests. The next time we would normally pick up a newspaper off the rack, or turn on the TV news, we can tune them out, turn them off, and take our lives back by making a stand on behalf of the Family of One.

After all, when you really look closely at all the experiences life has to offer, being in Oneness is as good as it gets. The communities that have this synergistic focus are the ones who will not only prosper, they will set the examples for all other groups to follow. Their lights will shine far and wide because they will have tasted the best that life has to offer.

And therein lies the result we're really looking for. Therein comes the feeling we have long sought and deserve. Therein is how we pass life's tests and move on to our next endeavor. Indeed, those who choose Oneness over separation, truth over lies, peace over war, and love over fear shall be the ones to bring forth a new way of life to all people everywhere. They will give birth to the Family of One.

When we stop asking ourselves "What's in it for me?" and start asking "What's in it for humanity as a whole?" the Family of One will awaken and will reveal Itself in all Its glory.

Our Invisible Community

As part of the great change that looms before us, we are shifting into a new dimension, a new world where we will meet all sorts of people and beings who are currently not seen by us while we are still focused on this 3-D world. Many of these beings may be scary, like some you see in sci-fi movies today, and others will be angelic and wanting to help us the minute we arrive.

Those who have attended my workshops and speaking events know that I always invoke angels and helpers from the invisible realms. Not only does it feel wonderful, it is part of the key to our evolution and to moving gracefully through the acceleration that is upon us. In order for us to evolve, we must learn that our invisible helpers reach out to us in the same measure that we are reaching out to them.

Three weeks ago, I was stretched out in my van outside Jeff's place in Key Largo about ten o'clock at night, getting ready to go to sleep. Trade winds blew gently through the trees above as the neighborhood quieted down for the night. As I often do when the timing seems right, I invoked the invisibles, firmly saying, "Here and Now, I Call Forth all of God's Holiest Angels and all of my Guardian Angels to intercede on behalf of the Highest Good for all of Humanity."

In that exact instant, the lights up and down the whole block went out! I can't tell you how good it felt. Within moments, my senses came alive. The nighttime sky—indeed, the whole of Nature—opened up before me as if to say, "Take a break. Be at Peace. Remember . . ."

The lights even stayed out for a couple of hours, and during that time I realized that was a message in itself. All of the buzzing transformers, power lines, lights, and electrical appliances had been having a subtle effect on all of us, distracting us from being able to focus well, keeping us jittery and busier than we needed to be. The quiet that ensued for those two hours was like a calm after the storm. The feeling was reminiscent of the twenty-six years I spent back in the hills of Hawaii, living far away from the grid.

The Masters are available from the inside.

CHAPTER 5

The Power Agreements

The experiences in my Intenders Circles have shown me that there are three agreements we can make with ourselves that will catapult us into our power right away. These three Power Agreements open the door for us to manifest anything we want:

1. I am unlimited in every way.

2. I am open to receive from unexpected sources.

3. I am unconcerned with what others think of me.

After eighteen years of seeing Intenders manifest their dreams and desires, we've found that those who are able to integrate these three Power Agreements into their lives tend to be the Mighty Manifestors. In rising up and out of their limitations and fears, they've tapped into something that evades others who haven't quite accessed their power yet.

The First Power Agreement

In making the first Power Agreement with ourselves, the Mighty Manifestors know that there are no limits. All of our limits are self-imposed, even though it may often appear otherwise. Likewise, we understand that it is we who make the final decision about whether we buy into a limiting belief or not. Others may try to persuade us that it's in our best interests to agree with a particular belief, but most often the person who is doing the persuading is not as aware of how the intention process works as we are.

Once upon a time, there was a gardener who had to leave her beautiful garden behind and start a new garden in a place where the soil was rocky, depleted of nutrients, and filled with weeds. Since she was a master manifestor as well as a master gardener, she knew to build her new garden in her mind first. In other words, she held a picture in her mind of the final outcome, of the way she wanted her garden to look when it was all done—and she did this before ever planting a seed or putting a shovel to the Earth.

In an effort to become familiar with which fruits, flowers, herbs, and vegetables grew best in her new locale, she began asking everyone in the area about gardening. She asked the neighbors who had nice gardens, and she queried the local university extension service as well. Most people wanted to help her, but many said that the piece of property where she was located was dead; that it was not a good place to grow a productive, organic garden. They had all sorts of reasons which sounded convincing. But there was one thing unconvincing about them: not one of them corresponded with the picture she had in her mind of the final outcome she was envisioning.

So she listened to the naysayers, but she didn't agree with them in the least. She knew that the key to manifesting was to hold steadfast to her vision and continue to see the garden in her mind as the healthiest, happiest, most productive garden she'd ever grown, knowing that these thoughts would work their way to the surface of her daily experience as surely as all her other thoughts did.

And you know what? They did. At the end of the season, people from all over the countryside were coming to see her beautiful gardens. She even won awards from the state horticultural society! And when they would ask her about her secret, "Is it the seeds? Or some special fertilizer? Or lots of hard work?" she just smiled and said, "I grew everything in my imagination first. Just because there were a lot of weeds for awhile, or folks who told me I couldn't do it, I never let that get in the way of the picture of the beautiful garden I had already grown in my mind."

The Second Power Agreement

The second Power Agreement suggests that we let go of predetermined ideas about how things will come to us, or where things will come from. Per the Fourth Intent of The Code, we have gleaned the wisdom in allowing things to come to us from anyone, anywhere. Whereas in the past, we may have harbored the thought that things can only come if we work hard, take out loans, make payments for years on end, or encumber ourselves in any number of ways, now we are expanding our horizons. We have learned from all of the success stories in our Intenders Circles to be ready and willing to receive our manifestations from all possible sources, and in doing so, we have opened the floodgates to our greatest abundance.

As we were riding around the northwest Oregon coast recently, my new friend, Terry, said that her manifestations were coming so fast now that she almost needed a stopwatch to be able to keep track of the minutes or seconds it took from the time she makes an intention to the time it manifests.

Throughout the day of driving, I noticed she was right. Just about everything she said happened right away! She commented on the heavy traffic and intended that the cars that were following us too closely move further away so that we had a buffer zone between us and the cars on all sides—and within seconds there weren't any cars anywhere to be seen. She intended parking spaces, friends to show up, a herd of elk, a camera when we needed one, and all of it came almost immediately! It was like riding around with a magician. Later on, she even intended that she have an eagle feather, and that same night a friend gave her one!

The most interesting thing about our day was that we acknowledged the flow we were in. We mentioned it to each other several times and simply took it for granted that whatever we wanted (as long as it was for the Highest Good) would come to us. And it did!

We even talked about how all of us are creating more instantaneously nowadays, and wouldn't it be a good idea if we were to give out Intenders Mighty Manifestor Stopwatches to people who had the fastest manifestations!

Looking back, the lesson in this story is not so much that we can manifest more quickly now (and it's going to be coming even quicker). The lesson is that we must always be open to receive from unexpected sources—and we must be very attentive to what it is that we are intending and make even surer that it is a creation that serves us and those around us. We really wouldn't want to continue manifesting situations that don't serve us anymore, would we?

The Third Power Agreement

The third Power Agreement dispels the fear of "what will people think of me?" and it allows us to step into our God-given power. When you look around our world, very few have had the courage to be different and go beyond this fear. Most go along with the crowd. But now, with the coming of the Great Shift, there are some who are not going along. There are some who are becoming very powerful.

Back in the nineteen-eighties, the lava flow from the southeast rift of Kilauea Volcano on the island of Hawaii poured over the magnificent Queen's Bath, destroying it entirely. One of the Earth's most beautiful secrets was gone forever. I used to play there in my youth, often having this lush, clear swimming hole all to myself.

Now, all you see is barren lava—except for one unusual area that stands out in the middle of the grey-black lava fields. Directly uphill from where the Queen's Bath used to be is a grove of tall coconut palms and an arrangement of rocks that the Hawaiians call a heiau, which means Hawaiian temple. One cannot help but notice it because there is no way anything should be living there. The lava flow is over a mile wide, and nothing survived except for the heiau.

The Hawaiians tell stories about how the Kahunas inter-vened with Madame Pele, the Goddess of the Volcano, and she spared this sacred place where so many prayers had been infused into the rocks in the past. Like the parting of the Red Sea, the river of approaching lava split in two just a few yards above the heiau and came back together when it had passed, missing the edges by only a few inches in many places.

The story of this sacred heiau reminds us of what we need to do nowadays to hold on to our power while the messages from the mainstream media continue to barrage us. As we said earlier, the consensus reality—the one that is constantly being pumped into us by the media—is but one reality out of an infinite number of realities in which we can choose to believe. We can keep our attention on it, or we can put our attention on another more comfortable, fulfill-ing reality. Whatever we place our attention on is what we are creating for ourselves. That is the Law.

As Intenders of the Highest Good, and as lightworkers who are beginning to gather our power at this time, we must be like the Kahunas who were completely undistracted by what others would have to say about them when they saved their beloved heiau from the fiery flow of lava. In this way, if the value of our money changes, or our comfort zones are being assaulted from all sides, we will stand strong in our power and continue to manifest to our heart's delight.

In order for you to go to the next level, you must unify with your higher self. Your higher self sees everything as if it were a play going on in your life. It sees things

from a higher place, as if you were standing on a
mountain top and looking down upon it all.

With the coming of a new world, everyone who has been working diligently with the Intention Process, the Law of Attraction, the Laws of Manifestation, or whatever you choose to call it, is finding that their manifesting skills are bearing fruit in seemingly miraculous ways. What this means is that those who are consciously giving a direction to their days, turning their doubts and unwanted thoughts around, being grateful for their experiences, intending truly to serve others, doing what they love to do, lining up with the Highest Good, and being trusting and open to receive will be receiving with greater ease and less effort than ever before. It's as if the doors to our greatest happiness and all that we have worked for are opening, never to close again.

This is the time we have been waiting for. We the People are coming into our power, and, from this point on, there is no stopping us. We will no longer be giving our power away to others who couldn't care less about us because *we have begun to realize that our internal world—what we think and how we feel—need not be dependent upon what is going on outside of us.* The constant media hype, as well as its reinforcement by our unawakened friends, is put in its rightful place along with all the other excess baggage we've let go of. Our power and our inner peace take precedence now, instead of our reliance upon outside forces and farces.

A word to the wise: those around you who are not choosing to explore their highest potentials and have not begun to familiarize themselves with the Laws of Manifestation are in for some challenging times. Since they have aligned themselves so closely with the mainstream matrix and all of its trappings, they will have to deal with greater and greater states of discomfort and you will see this all around you. However, it is for you to retain your poise and remain uplifted no matter what is going on in your external world. That is how you set an example for others to follow. That is your job in these challenging times: to stay positive, to shine your light, and to bring others up to where you are.

All the things you are seeking are inside of you.

CHAPTER 6

The 2012 Agreement

From the level of our soul, we all made agreements to be here at this time. Our job is to usher in a new way of life, an entirely new reality. Like midwives, we are here to help in giving birth to a golden age of manifestation upon the Earth.

At the same time, the current world acceleration is requiring us to adapt to challenges and situations we never expected to have to deal with. Many of us got caught up in the ways of the old paradigm. However, now that our purpose here is being revealed to us, we find that, in order to bring forth a new world, we must first be willing to let go of the current mainstream matrix with all of its same old tricks. For some people this will be easy. But for others, it may be a bit of a rocky road. Our success lies in our ability to trust our intuition, our common sense, and our conscience to guide us through it all.

It always seems strange to me that when I go to a sporting event in a large stadium and they play the national anthem, almost everyone in the crowd stands up and supposedly holds their hand over their heart, off to the side of their chest. The same thing happens when you go into a classroom today and see the children saying the Pledge of Allegiance to the flag while holding their hands over a spot on the side of their chests, thinking that is where their heart is.

But wait a minute! That's not where our heart is at all. Our heart is in the exact center of our chest. No matter what the doctors, teachers, sports enthusiasts, or children tell you, your heart is in the middle, just as if your body was aligned on a cross. The exact center point where the horizontal and vertical points meet is where the heart of your heart sits. I've even spoken with young children about this, and they will swear that their heart is off-center. When I asked them how they knew that to be true, they said that their teacher told them so.

So what is the purpose in deceiving so many people from a very young age about the correct placement of their heart? It is because our heart is a very special focal point. It is where we connect to all the Love in the Universe. However, if we can't find it, or think it is somewhere it isn't, then it becomes harder for us to come into contact with the true Love of God. And it is much easier for us to be controlled.

It sounds crazy, but on a very subtle level, when we lose track of the location of our heart, it becomes more difficult for us to send and receive Love. For thousands of years the powers that be have conspired to keep our hearts hidden from us so they could keep us anchored to the Earth where it is easier to manipulate us. But now we are beginning to see through all of the deceptions that are constantly being perpetrated upon humanity, and we are finding our hearts and all the Love that resides there. For it is in the center of our heart where all of the things we search for, where all of the treasures we travel far and wide to find, where all of the successes we toil for lifetimes to achieve, and where the most sacred sites and the sweetest feelings available to us can be found. For those who are still skeptical, I suggest that you hold *your undivided attention on the center of your chest for awhile and see what happens.*

Many things will be surfacing that have been hidden. Many discoveries will be made—discoveries of other worlds, other ways, other civilizations—that have been here on this planet.

As I have said, the change that is upon us is one of *perception*. Our perceptions are being enhanced, our intuitions are awakening, our third eyes are dilating, our hearts are opening. It is a change of consciousness, of the way we look at the world, of the world itself appearing fundamentally different to us than it does today.

We are shifting into another dimension and, when the dust settles, life will be akin to the feeling you had when you were young; playing with your neighborhood friends around sunset, and your mother calling out and saying that it was time for you to come inside. You were having so much fun. . . . Then your mother remembered there wasn't any school tomorrow, so she yelled out from the back door that you and your friends could stay out and play for as long as you like. Remember that? Having so much fun that you didn't want it to end—ever? That's the way life is supposed to be, and that is *the feeling* the new world offers to us.

As part of the speeding up that is going on as we move into 2012 and the Great Shift that stands before us, we will be going through several critical masses, several tipping points. Each of these tipping points will be accompanied by a breakthrough that leads us ever closer to the Big Tipper where we really begin to love one another again, where we really honor each other, regardless of our differences, and where we truly experience the totality of the Family of One.

Each of these tipping points will bring a huge feeling of relief and release from our fear and suffering. For instance, as we all agree upon the wisdom in helping instead of harming one another, we will tip into a better place. The Earth will suddenly be a more comfortable environment for us to live in.

Another tipping point will be when we see the great advantage in not carrying weapons of all kinds because we will have realized, by the Law of Attraction, that we are inviting an attack upon us when we seek to defend ourselves. Indeed, we will realize that it is the thought of being attacked that causes us to carry weapons and protect ourselves in the first place, and we will set all our weapons aside because our common sense has reawakened and shown us, ever so clearly, that we really wouldn't want to be attracting an attack; that it would be better, by far, to put all the guns, bombs, and weapons away and see what that's like. That day will bring forth a huge tipping point for us.

Likewise, when we see the depth of the deceptions perpetrated upon us, we will eventually tip because we will say, "I've had it! No longer will I support anyone who is robbing me of my energy. No longer will I lend my *agreement* to anyone who is harming the Earth and Her people." When enough of us have proclaimed this and the paradigm of pain comes to an end, it will precipitate a glorious new tipping point for all of mankind.

A Potential Progression of Tipping Points

1. When today's leaders confess to what they've done;
2. When the fighting stops everywhere;
3. When all toxic dumping and chemtrails stop;
4. When all debts are forgiven;
5. When Greenwich Mean Time is abandoned;
6. When we line up collectively for the Highest Good;
7. When the world's religions come together;
8. When all man-made boundaries are erased;
9. When we truly love, honor, and respect each other;
10. When all hearts are opened;
11. When the Family of One is made manifest;
12. When we see a bigger cosmological picture;
13. When the invisible becomes visible;
14. When we wake up, one day, in a completely new world.

Soon, there will come a time when these tipping points come faster and closer together, and we will have insight after insight after insight in such a short period of time that we can barely imagine it from where we stand today. As this is being written, it appears to many like it is still "business as usual," but you can be assured that the world a few years from now will be vastly different. *Things happen very fast at the end of a cycle.*

To get a rough idea of how the last days of our old culture will proceed, we would need to understand how exponential growth, or doubling, works because it shows us how things happen faster at the end of civilizations and cycles. Exponential growth is a fascinating phenomenon that occurs as things double in size at a steady rate.

To better understand exponential growth, let's consider an example. Let's suppose that there is a jar filled with marbles. The number of marbles in the jar is doubling every day, and in thirty days the jar will be full. Now . . . just for the fun of it, here is a puzzle for you: if the marbles are doubling every day, and the jar is full on the thirtieth day, on what day is the jar half full?

On the twenty-ninth day, right? You got it.

So here's the next puzzle: on which day is the jar one quarter full?

You got it again: on the twenty-eighth day. Here's the point: if you were a marble inside that jar on the twenty-eighth day and you looked around, it wouldn't appear to be too crowded yet, would it? It would seem like you have plenty of time to do all the things you'd like to do, right? But, actually, in just two days the jar is going to be full—and only a handful of astute marbles can see what's going on. Something's got to give.

This is what is happening in our world today. Our population is doubling at an unprecedented rate, our infrastructures are crumbling commensurately, and most people know something's speeding up, but they don't want things to change. No matter how bad it gets. As in our example above, something's got to give, and it's our current way of life that must give way to a new way of living.

That's why we have brought The Intenders Circle format, The Intention Process, the Highest Light Teachings, and *The Code* to the peoples of the world at this time. These tools are meant to help us through the Great Shift and to act as guidelines while the changes are upon us, and beyond. They have been put into place to be used at a time when they are needed most. *That time is now.* Indeed, when enough people see what is happening and intend, firmly, that they are going to live in a new way, refraining from harming and opposing one another, setting their weapons aside, protecting our precious resources, working to clean up Mother Earth, teaching their children new values, and coming together on behalf of the whole of humanity, then we will tip.

As the population doubles, so does the number of people who are waking up, as does the number of people who take a stand for the Highest Good. Both the population and the number of people who are carrying light are expanding exponentially at the same time—but hold it a minute! *There's a wild card in the mix!*

The Universe as a whole is raising its frequency. It's raising its vibration and readying for a tipping point of its own. A transformation is upon us as light floods into areas of the entire cosmos that have been consumed and ruled by the dark for eons. The veil is being lifted, and it's not going to matter how the population grows or the infrastructure crumbles because a new world is coming—and with it also comes the ability for us to work directly with light to clean up the chaos, clean up the waters, clean up our old habits, and lift our arms to the sky in gratitude for the grace of God.

One day, in the near future—*in our lifetimes*—we will stand together in awe of what we have witnessed. For we will have taken part in the most extraordinary transformational experience available to anyone, in any dimension, anywhere.

And we will have remembered why we came here. For, in rising from the darkest depths of despair to the highest of heights, there is no experience in all of creation that we could have chosen to be a part of that is as good as this one.

You have known before you came here that there would be a time when you would be called upon. It is a time for you to follow Spirit without hesitation and to live in the light on a daily basis. That time, which you have long awaited, has come.

Epilogue

As we wind down on our discussion about the Law of Agreement, let's chat for a moment about the common man and woman. You and me. The common man and woman want peace. We want to live our lives free from the agendas and dark dealings of those who currently rule this planet. In fact, the common man and woman are beginning to see through all of the deceptive practices employed by the Earth's rulers, and we are looking for something new, something we can put our faith in, and trust, without a doubt, that our best interests are served.

The common man and woman are open, now more than ever, for a voice that speaks not about enemies but about making friends; not about terror, but love; not about fear, but a rising up and out of fear into the light of a new day, where all of us can breathe a collective sigh of relief because the reign of our beautiful Mother Earth has been handed over to people who deeply care about their fellow travelers.

The days of *agreeing* with contrived oppositions, where we are pitted against one another, are fast coming to a close. The common man and woman have had enough. We are rejecting the same old tricks, withholding our agreement from obvious contrivances that call for defending ourselves or attacking others. We are realizing, clearly now, that opposing another will not give us the results we are looking for.

Nothing less than a true and lasting peace will be accepted. Nothing less than working toward that which connects us, instead of that which separates us, will be honored. The senseless practice of placing our warriors up on pedestals and treating them like our greatest heroes is passing away, as we begin to see, with the greatest of clarity, that our truest heroes are the ones who stand up for the Highest Good of all—not just the Highest Good of the contradictory few.

Our guiding light in these times is the Highest Good. It is our saving grace, our beacon pointing the way into a safe harbor where the waters are calm and the people are filled with an expectation of great things to come. The Highest Good. Think about it. It offers us the promise of a world where we are all truly equal, where we are all seen for the spark of magnificence within, and where none are mistreated or left by the wayside.

We have been led to believe that we have no other options; that we must put up with present-day rulers and leaders who are completely devoid of conscience; that we must forever live in a world where killing and suffering continue unabated. But this is simply not true, and it isn't for our Highest Good. It is in the Highest Good that each and every man, woman, and child who treads this Earth is given free rein to lovingly pursue his or her total fulfillment without interruption or distraction.

Change is imminent. The days of waiting and procrastinating are over. The Highest Good is calling, now, for us to bring forth a world of love, a world where we look back upon these chaotic times and thank our lucky stars that they are finally over because we woke up and said, "Enough!" We no longer *agree* with anyone who would advocate anything less than complete and lasting peace for all mankind.

That future stands before us, still as bright and shining as it ever was. We need only consider the Highest Good and It will take us there.

When you give your agreement to that which is good, you just make more of it.

A Parting Reminder

Everything you need is here for you. You need only look around to see that this is true. The trees offer shade from the sun, block the wind in times of storms, make perches for the little birds to sing you their songs, and provide their wood for building your shelters. The animals offer loving companionship and comfort when you are alone. They pull your plows, run your races, fetch your food, and even offer their own bodies so that yours may be sustained. What more could you ask of them?

Your friends and enemies alike fill your life with every kind of experience. They dance with you, sing with you, work with you, love with you. Without them, you would not want to be here. Even your opponents present you with opportunities for growth and regeneration. For it is a great truth that every time you forgive another, you are rejuvenated. Every time you turn an unloving relationship around, you are refreshed and renewed.

Your brothers and sisters with whom you walk this Earth are gifts unto you, each one bringing something new, something you need for your own fulfillment. Even Mother Earth, Herself, laughs as you laugh, cries as you cry, cheers when you cheer. She is with you always, in Her heart, and in yours.

All of life supports you. There is not a rock, a branch, a hillside, a drop or an ocean of water that turns away as you approach. All are here for you to work with, to play with, to commune with, to create and recreate with. The world is a joyous playground offering itself for you to do with as you please. There is only one rule of thumb you need follow: *Take care of it.* Take care of it all, so it can thrive and enjoy its experience fully and freely.

Take care of it, so it can, in turn, take care of you.

Acknowledgments

My deepest gratitude goes to six amazing women whose support for my work has been above and beyond anything I could have ever imagined: Vicki Harding, Tina Stober, Betsy Palmer Whitney, Pam Baugh, Sarah Brown, and Alva Kamalani—goddesses, one and all! Thank you!

The Code:
10 Intentions for a Better World

The First Intent: Support Life

I refrain from opposing or harming anyone. I allow others to have their own experiences. I see life in all things and honor it as if it were my own. I support life.

The Second Intent: Seek Truth

I follow my inner compass and discard any beliefs that are no longer serving me. I go to the source. I seek truth.

The Third Intent: Set Your Course

I begin the creative process. I give direction to my life. I set my course.

The Fourth Intent: Simplify

*I let go so there is room for something better to come in.
I intend that I am guided, guarded, protected, and lined
up with the Highest Good at all times. I trust and remain
open to receive from both expected and unexpected
sources. I simplify.*

The Fifth Intent: Stay Positive

*I see good, say good, and do good. I accept the gifts from
all of my experiences. I am living in grace and gratitude.
I stay positive.*

The Sixth Intent: Synchronize

*After intending and surrendering, I take action by following
the opportunities that are presented to me. I am in the flow
where Great Mystery and Miracles abide, fulfilling my
desires and doing what I came here to do. I synchronize.*

The Seventh Intent: Serve Others

*I practice love in action. I always have enough to spare
and enough to share. I am available to help those who
need it. I serve others.*

The Eighth Intent: Shine Your Light

I am a magnificent being, awakening to my highest potential. I express myself with joy, smiling easily and laughing often. I shine my light.

The Ninth Intent: Share Your Vision

I create my ideal world by envisioning it and telling others about it. I share my vision.

The Tenth Intent: Synergize

I see Humanity as One. I enjoy gathering with lighthearted people regularly. When we come together, we set the stage for Great Oneness to reveal Itself. We synergize.

About The Intenders of
the Highest Good

If you are seeking to be part of a community of like-minded and lighthearted people who are becoming empowered and lined up with the Highest Good at the same time, The Intenders is open to everyone. You can visit our website at *www.intenders.com* to see if there is an Intenders Circle already near you. Or if you would like to start your own Circle, our Create Your Own Community Package makes it easy for you.

To contact us:
Visit: *www.intenders.com*
Email: office@intenders.com
Phone: (888) 422-2420

If you would like to know more about the Intention Process or the finer points of the Laws of Manifestation, we recommend The Intenders Bridge, our uplifting daily email program, which is available at *www.intenders.org.*

Likewise, if you are intending to truly make a difference in our world, you can sign up for The Vision Alignment Project at *www.visionalignmentproject.com* and align with our ideal visions. Both The Intenders Bridge and The Vision Alignment Project are free and are also available at *www.intenders.com*.

You can download a free 8 x 11 poster of *The Code* at *www.intenders.com/TheCode.html*—or order an 11 x 17 color poster of *The Code* from our website. *The Code: 10 Intentions for a Better World* is published by Weiser Books and is available at bookstores everywhere.

About the Author

Tony Burroughs is one of our greatest storytellers. As cofounder of The Intenders of the Highest Good and author of *The Code*, most of his time is spent traveling, bringing people together in Intention Circles, and helping them become more proficient at using the Laws of Manifestation. He calls Pagosa Springs, Colorado his home.

To Our Readers